D0927021

THE TASHA TUDOR
COOKBOOK

THE TASHA TUDOR
COOKBOOK

Recipes and Reminiscences from Corgi Cottage

Written and illustrated by
TASHA TUDOR

with Carol Johnston Lueck

LITTLE, BROWN AND COMPANY
Boston New York Toronto London

Copyright © 1993 by Tasha Tudor

All rights reserved. No part of this book may be reproduced in any
form or by any electronic or mechanical means, including
information storage and retrieval systems, except by a
reviewer who may quote brief passages
in a review.

First Edition

Library of Congress Cataloging-in-Publication Data
Tudor, Tasha.
    The Tasha Tudor cookbook : recipes and reminiscences
from Corgi Cottage / written and illustrated by Tasha Tudor.
— 1st ed.
        p.   cm.
    Includes index.
    ISBN 0-316-85531-6
    1. Cookery, American — New England style. I. Title.
TX715.2.N48T83   1993
641.5974 — dc20   93-16438

10 9 8 7 6 5 4 3 2 1

TWP

Designed by Barbara Werden

Published simultaneously in Canada by
Little, Brown & Company (Canada) Limited

Printed in Singapore

*To all my nice fans, to whom I owe
a large debt of gratitude.*
Tasha Tudor

To all my dear family.
Carol Johnston Lueck

Table of Contents

Preface

Cooking is one of my favorite occupations, especially when I have my appreciative family on hand to praise my efforts.

My Scottish nanny, Mary Burnett ("Dady" to me), started me early in the pleasures of the culinary art; I can hardly remember when I didn't cook. I guess my first productions were sun-baked mudpies. My daughters were more fortunate in that they had a tame crow, Edgar Allen Crow, who *ate* their mud pies with avid enthusiasm. He was a delightful bird who highly approved of mudpie cakes decorated with nasturtiums in particular.

Serious meal preparation started for me at around age fourteen, when my mother bought an eighteenth-century home in Redding, Connecticut. She spent many hours scouring the countryside in her Franklin Touring car, searching for wide boards, paneling, and twenty-four-pane window sashes with handblown glass with which to restore the house to its former glory. I recall her buying three-foot cedar "shakes" from the birthplace of the famous Tom Thumb in Bridgeport, Connecticut. This left me to cook for my brother Frederic, nine years my senior, and the Deming boys, Benton and

Olcott, all employed in restoring the old home, haying the fields, and digging numberless deep holes for the telephone poles, made from dead chestnut trees cut by a neighbor, Clarence Beers. They had ravenous appetites, so I became the cook and turned out Irish stew and vast quantities of homemade bread and rolls. It was excellent practice.

From this I went on to helping my mother run a tea room that she started in the restored house. I baked endless cakes, cookies, and breads. Such fun — especially as I was able to earn money from tips since I was the only waitress!

I became quite "stuck-up" about my breadmaking and actually won a blue ribbon for my whole wheat bread at the Danbury Fair. "Dady" taught me how to make real Scottish shortbread and, of course, Yorkshire Pudding and scones, plus cakes, pies, and cookies of all sorts.

I soon began earning money by selling breads and cakes to neighbors and at the weekly Redding market. The proceeds from these sales were the start of my 1830 clothing collection. Besides her tea room, my mother also had an antique business, which led to her attending many auctions. Whenever possible, I went with her, and often I got away with shocking bargains, as nobody wanted to bid against "that quaint little girl"! Times have changed, and so have I, but the lure of a good antiques show is as strong as ever for this "quaint old woman" (but no more bargains, alas!).

The receipts (I was taught to spell them in this fashion) in this book form a record gathered from many resources, mostly of family origin and dating as far back as the 1700s. They were copied by hand into a blank "dummy" of many years back. All four of my children, two girls and two boys, learned to cook from this book, now very worn, stained, and tattered from devoted use. It is held together by a delightfully pliant string, made so by butter and flour on young fingers. The pages that contained the favorite receipts can be easily found by their spots and spills.

In making these receipts I have had the good fortune of having access to the freshest eggs, homemade butter, goat's milk, and an abundance of garden-fresh vegetables. I even had my own flour ground from wheat that I had planted and threshed myself. I hope the readers who try these receipts will have the pleasure and success for their efforts that I have had. I want to stress the importance of using the freshest possible ingredients, and in soups and stews of tasting, tasting, tasting for seasoning. A flat soup is a real disappointment. And don't look for shortcuts; all good and worthwhile things take time and effort.

I am indebted to my friend Carol Johnston Lueck, who diligently tested the receipts. She even learned to use a computer in the process! I compliment her on deciphering my handwriting and on being able to figure out exact measurements for the ingredients — a real task, as I use my imagination in all my cooking. Thanks, too, to my kind friends who have been willing to share some of their receipts with me. Thanks also to my agent, Colleen Mohyde, for her enthusiasm for the entire project, and to my editor, Jennifer Josephy, for her fine work in getting *The Tasha Tudor Cookbook* into print.

Good luck!

TASHA TUDOR
Corgi Cottage
1993

APPETIZERS
AND
SALADS

Nancy's Hot Cheese Rounds

Nancy Smith was a dear friend and the wife of the mathematics teacher at Saint Paul's School. She was an expert hostess and entertained all the renowned parents who visited their offspring at Saint Paul's. Her Hot Cheese Rounds are, I assure you, outstanding before an elegant dinner party or a holiday feast.

My grandfather Tudor was one of the first students at Saint Paul's, in the 1860s. He spoke of the water's being frozen in the wash pitchers on cold winter mornings! He took it quite for granted, too. I cannot see a modern youth taking such a hardship with equanimity, can you?

1 loaf Pepperidge Farm or other good-quality
   white bread
$1/_2$ cup (1 stick) unsalted butter, softened
1 3-ounce package cream cheese, softened
1 farm-fresh egg yolk, beaten well
1 cup Vermont sharp cheddar cheese, grated
1 clove garlic, minced
salt and pepper

Heat the broiler.

Cut the bread into rounds with a biscuit cutter. (I feed the leftover crusts to the hens for a treat.) Butter the rounds well and fry them on both sides in a hot skillet until delicately brown. Cool.

In a bowl, cream together the cream cheese and the egg yolk, then add the grated cheese, garlic, and salt and pepper to taste.

Spread the cheese mixture on the rounds, taking care to spread it carefully to the edges so the toast does not burn. Put the rounds on a baking sheet and place it under the heated broiler until the cheese is puffed and browned. Keep a sharp eye on the rounds while broiling.

Serve immediately.

Makes approximately 2 dozen

Stuffed Eggs

Stuffed eggs are a necessity for a memorable picnic. I learned to make them during summers spent in Nahant, Massachusetts, with Jeanie Paine, my oldest friend. She attended my first birthday, and I hers. We were the fourth generation of friends in the Paine and Burgess families. Her children and mine are now the fifth. The Paines' Irish cook packed the eggs for us to take to the beach, a magical place with rocks, caves, and fascinating tide pools in which Jeanie and I floated whole flotillas of mussel-shell merchant and pirate ships.

12 farm-fresh eggs
salt and pepper to taste
1 cup Hellmann's mayonnaise
3 tablespoons French Dressing (page 6)
1/2 cup mixed fresh-picked herbs, such as thyme, marjoram, sweet ciceley, tarragon, chives, summer savory, winter savory, parsley, and mint
2 or 3 garlic cloves, minced
parsley or paprika for garnish

Boil the eggs gently for 20 minutes, then drain and run cold water over them. Peel when cool. (Eggs that were laid 3 or 4 days before peel the best; really fresh eggs are difficult to peel. Bantam eggs are especially nice to use for garnishing salads because they are only half the size of regular hen's eggs. Hard-boiled turkey eggs can cause a real sensation!) Cut the eggs in half lengthwise. Put the yolks in a bowl and place the empty whites on a plate.

Mash the yolks with a fork; then add the salt, pepper, mayonnaise, French dressing, herbs, and garlic. *Mix well*, until light and fluffy, and fill each half egg white with the mixture. (You may pipe it in with a pastry tube if you wish to be fancy.) Sprinkle the stuffed eggs with finely chopped parsley or paprika.

Serves 6

Fresh Tomato Salad

Sun-ripened tomatoes grown in your own garden are naturally the best and most flavorful kind. This is a wonderful salad to serve with sliced cold meats. The tomatoes are also very pretty encircling a plate of potato or chicken salad and make a very tasty addition.

Tomatoes should never be placed in the refrigerator; they should always be kept at room temperature.

To peel tomatoes easily, place them in a pot of boiling water for ten to fifteen seconds before peeling.

4 medium tomatoes, picked fresh from the garden
1/2 teaspoon fresh basil, chopped
4 tablespoons French Dressing (page 6)

Peel and slice fresh garden tomatoes about 1/4 inch thick and place the slices on a pretty serving plate.

Pour French dressing over all and sprinkle with basil.

Allow to stand to enhance the flavor.

Serves 4

French Dressing

One of my favorite specialties, this dressing enhances all salads. The addition of fresh herbs makes for an unusually tasty dressing. Nearly all my receipts require a garden of culinary herbs, which poses a problem, but windowsill or half-barrel gardening can be delightful. Try it!

1/2 cup olive oil
1/8 cup cider vinegar
1 small yellow onion, peeled
3 cloves garlic, peeled
3 tablespoons ketchup
1 teaspoon sugar
salt and pepper to taste
1 tablespoon Colman's dry mustard
a few drops of Tabasco sauce
*a few drops of Lea & Perrins Worcestershire
    sauce*
*thyme, chervil, tarragon, and basil (added for
    flavor—do not chop)*

Combine all the ingredients in a covered pint jar. Shake well and keep at room temperature until serving time.

Remove the onion and herbs before pouring the dressing on salad.

Makes approximately 1 cup

Avocado and Grapefruit Salad

This is a simple and delicate salad for serving at any time of the year. It makes any meal special. We often take it along on picnics in a small crock, and serve it with macaroni and cheese in the wintertime.

1 grapefruit
½ small onion
3 tablespoons French Dressing (page 6)
1 ripe avocado, cubed
1 head Boston lettuce

Peel the grapefruit and carefully separate and cut out the sections, placing them in a bowl. Strain off the juice. Mince the onion and add it to the grapefruit. Stir in the French dressing and let stand for an hour.

Just before serving, add the avocado and mix well.

Serve on crisp green Boston lettuce leaves.

Serves 4

Potato Salad

Every June, on Midsummer's Eve, we hold a splendid celebration known as the Stillwater Party. Stillwater is the name thought up by my younger son and me for a mock New England sect combining Shaker, Amish, and Quaker qualities. The Stillwaters believe that life should be enjoyed and appreciated and Nature revered.

The party is always a joyous and impressive event, complete with a barn dance set to fiddle and accordion music supplied by talented friends; a marionette show put on either by our family or by professional friends; and a truly sumptuous repast, including this potato salad. Neighbors contribute all sorts of delectable salads, breads, cakes, cookies, and so on. And we try to have goat ice cream, to which nothing can compare.

I mix this salad just before a party, for it tastes best at room temperature.

8 medium potatoes
6 farm-fresh eggs
6 cloves garlic,
    pressed
1 large onion,
    finely chopped
8 slices cooked bacon
1 cup Hellmann's
    mayonnaise

¹/₄ cup plain white vinegar
¹/₂ cup French Dressing (page 6)
¹/₂ cup fresh dill, thyme, summer savory, or
    parsley, or a combination, finely chopped
1 head Boston lettuce

Boil the potatoes and the eggs together in a pot. When the potatoes can be pierced with a fork, drain the liquid. Immediately peel the hot potatoes and chop them into ¹/₂-inch cubes. Peel the eggs and chop them. Add the eggs, garlic, onion, and crumbled bacon to the potatoes.

Add the mayonnaise, vinegar, and French dressing. Mix well. Add the chopped herbs and mix in.

Place Boston lettuce leaves on a serving platter and spoon the potato salad on top. Serve right away.

Serves 8

The Tasha Tudor Cookbook

Chicken Salad

This is another dish that is made in large quantities for the summer Stillwater Party. If you wish, you may roast the chicken a day in advance, chill it, and then cut it up the following day. This makes for less work on the day you entertain. Garnish with nasturtium flowers or violets, if you have some. Rose petals are also nice.

1 chicken, roasted (page 54)
4 farm-fresh eggs, hard boiled
1 1/2 cups fresh peas, cooked
2 celery ribs, chopped
2 onions, finely chopped
4 cloves garlic, pressed
1 cup Hellmann's mayonnaise
1/2 cup French Dressing (page 6)
1 cup or more fresh mixed herbs, such as
*   thyme, tarragon, sweet marjoram, chives,*
*   summer savory, or parsley, finely chopped*
salt and pepper to taste

1 head Boston lettuce
Fresh Tomato Salad (page 5)

Skin the roasted chicken and cut it into large cubes. Slice the eggs and add them to the chicken along with all the remaining ingredients except the salt and pepper, lettuce, and tomato salad. Mix well. Be sure to add enough dressing; do not skimp. Salt and pepper to taste—and do be sure to taste.

Arrange the lettuce leaves on a large platter, put the chicken salad mixture in the center, and surround with sliced tomatoes. I also use hard-boiled bantam eggs, stuffed, as a garnish.

Serves 6 to 8

SOUPS

Corgi Cottage Soup

I love to make soup and can say with pride that I am famous for it. This is a real winter standby if you live in a cold climate. I make a large iron potful at least once a week, either on the wood stove or over the fire, which burns all winter.

You must make this soup with a fresh farm chicken carcass, however. Those poor pallid birds that come from a supermarket just do not have enough flavor, so try to obtain a good farm-raised chicken. Roast it and enjoy it for dinner. When the chicken is eaten, put the carcass into the soup kettle and follow the receipt.

Stock:
1 chicken carcass
2 large onions, quartered
2 carrots, cut into large chunks
2 celeriac roots, peeled and cut into large
*   chunks*
6 cloves of garlic, minced
5 bay leaves
1 tablespoon chopped fresh parsley
1 teaspoon chopped fresh thyme

1 teaspoon chopped fresh sweet basil
1/2 teaspoon chopped fresh tarragon
salt and pepper to taste

1 cup frozen or fresh lima beans
2 cups frozen peas and carrots
2/3 cup white rice, uncooked
2/3 cup elbow macaroni, uncooked
1 receipt Mashed Potatoes (page 62)
1 28-ounce can B&M baked beans, with
*   salt pork removed*
1 or 2 Knorr's chicken bouillon cubes
1 large potato, grated (optional)
salt and pepper to taste
2 teaspoons each fresh chopped parsley,
*   oregano, tarragon, and sage*

Place the chicken carcass and all of the ingredients for the stock in a large stockpot. Bring to a boil and then simmer all day long, 6 to 7 hours. At the end of this time, remove the chicken carcass and strain the broth.

Place the frozen vegetables in a small pot, cover with water, and bring to a boil.

Add the rice and elbow macaroni and cook until tender, adding more water as needed. Continue to cook slowly until all of the water is boiled away, then add the vegetables, rice, and macaroni to the stock.

While the vegetables are cooking, make the receipt for mashed potatoes. These will be the thickener for the soup.

Pour some of the broth from the soup into the mashed potatoes, stirring to keep the mixture smooth. Stir this mixture into the soup broth and add the baked beans. Be careful not to let the soup scorch, as potatoes burn easily. Crumble in the chicken bouillon cubes.

If the soup is not thick enough, add 1 large raw potato, grated, and simmer for a bit.

Taste and add salt, pepper, and small amounts of chopped fresh herbs, as you desire, taking care not to add too much tarragon.

Serves 12

Cream of Mushroom Soup

This soup always brings to mind the overcast yet warm fall days in Redding, Connecticut, when my mother and I would roam over huge pastures hunting for field mushrooms, puffballs, inky caps, and even morels. I would suggest that you purchase your mushrooms from the market, a less romantic but safer alternative, if you cannot identify field mushrooms.

½ pound mushrooms, chopped
2 slices onion
2 tablespoons (¼ stick) unsalted butter
4 cups chicken stock
¼ cup quick tapioca
1 cup boiling water
salt and pepper to taste
1 cup cream
2 egg yolks, beaten slightly

Sauté the mushrooms and onion in the butter, then transfer to a stockpot, add the chicken stock, and simmer for half an hour. Strain through a sieve. Add the tapioca and boiling water. Simmer 10 minutes. Season as you like.

Just before serving, add the cream and egg yolks. Heat thoroughly, taking care *not to allow soup to boil.* Serve immediately.

Serves 6 to 8

Pea Soup

Invariably this scrumptious soup followed the event of a ham dinner. I associate it with cold days in midwinter and the welcome warmth of the open fire, where I often make it to this day. It is made in a large cast-iron pot that hangs from the crane. It needs frequent stirring to prevent its sticking, due to the intense heat put forth by a hardwood fire.

2 cups split green peas
2 quarts cold water
1 cup yellow onions, chopped
3 carrots, chopped
3 ribs celery (with leaves), chopped
1 meaty ham bone
salt and pepper to taste

Wash and sort the peas, then place them in a large soup kettle. Add the cold water and cover with a lid. Bring to a boil, then reduce heat and simmer for a minute or two. Remove from heat and allow to stand for 1 hour.

Add the vegetables and heat to boiling, then reduce heat and simmer, covered, for $2\frac{1}{2}$ hours, until the peas are tender. You may add the ham bone midway through the cooking time. When the peas are tender, remove the meat and allow it to cool before dicing. Strain the soup through a colander, then add the diced ham and season to taste with salt and pepper.

Serves 8 to 10

Potato and Onion Soup

A just-right soup to serve for lunch with Cornbread (page 36) and a salad. It never fails to bring praise for the cook from delighted guests and has the added advantage of being easily made ahead of time and reheated with no trouble.

6 tablespoons (³/₄ stick) unsalted butter,
   divided
3 cups onions or fresh leeks, minced
3 tablespoons flour
4 to 5 cups hot water
4 cups potatoes, cubed
salt and pepper to taste
1¹/₂ to 2 cups milk
¹/₂ cup heavy cream
chopped fresh parsley for garnish

In a 3-quart soup kettle, melt 3 tablespoons of the butter over moderate heat. Stir in the onions or leeks, cover the pot, and cook slowly for 5 minutes, stirring occasionally to prevent scorching. Next, whisk in the flour and stir over moderate heat for 2 minutes to cook the flour without browning.

Remove the kettle from the heat and cool a moment. Then gradually beat in 1 cup of hot water with a whisk, blending thoroughly. Stir in the remainder of the water. Stir in the potatoes and salt and pepper to taste. Bring to a boil, then simmer, partially covered, for 40 minutes, until the potatoes are tender.

Remove the soup from the heat. Strain the potatoes, returning the liquid to the soup kettle. Mash the potatoes and add them to the kettle. With a wooden spoon, stir in the milk, cream, and remaining butter. Taste for correct seasoning.

Serve very hot in soup cups and sprinkle each with a little bit of chopped fresh parsley.

Serves 8

Cream of Spinach Soup

I use leftover fresh-cooked spinach to make this cream soup; you may, however, use frozen spinach and precook it before you begin the receipt. I know that some people make croutons in the oven, but they cannot compare in flavor to croutons toasted in real butter in a frying pan on the stove.

1 1/2 cups cooked spinach, or 1 package frozen,
  cooked according to directions on package
3 cups fresh whole milk
2 tablespoons (1/4 stick) unsalted butter
1 onion, chopped
1 clove garlic, minced
2 tablespoons unbleached flour
1/2 Knorr's beef bouillon cube
salt and pepper to taste
1/8 teaspoon mace
croutons for garnish (receipt follows)

Blend the cooked spinach and milk in a blender. Place in the top of a double boiler to warm.

In an iron skillet, melt the butter and sauté the onion and garlic. Stir in the flour. Add the spinach mixture and stir well. Crumble some of the bouillon cube into the spinach, stirring well to dissolve. Season to taste with salt, pepper, and mace. (You may not need much salt, if any, as the bouillon cube is salty.)

Do not allow the soup to come to a boil. Serve immediately while still piping hot, topped with croutons.

Serves 4

Croutons

2 tablespoons (1/4 stick) unsalted butter
2 thin slices homemade white bread or
  Pepperidge Farm white bread, cubed

In a 6-inch iron skillet, melt the butter. Add the bread cubes and carefully brown on all sides, turning frequently to avoid scorching. When nicely browned and crisp, remove from the heat. Keep the croutons warm until the soup is ready to serve.

Add the croutons to the soup just as you serve it.

Vegetable Soup

This is a very delicate soup that I make for Thanksgiving and Christmas to serve as a first course. With the soup, I serve clover-leaf rolls made with the Rolls for Special Occasions dough (page 29).

5 tablespoons unsalted butter
1/2 cup carrot, diced
1/2 cup turnip, diced

1/2 cup celery, diced
1/2 cup potatoes, diced
1/2 small onion, cut in thin slices
1 clove garlic, minced
1 quart water
2 tablespoons fresh parsley, chopped
1 teaspoon sweet basil, chopped
1 teaspoon thyme
1 teaspoon tarragon
salt and pepper to taste

In a heavy stockpot, melt the butter. Add the diced vegetables and minced garlic and sauté for 10 minutes. Add the water and the herbs, bring to a boil, then lower the heat to medium and cook until the vegetables are tender, 30 to 45 minutes. Season to taste.

Serves 8 to 10

Nanny T.'s Fish Chowder

Whenever I make this delectable chowder, I see my nice round grandmother seated at the head of her perfectly set table, the large Canton soup tureen, silver soup ladle, and Canton chowder bowls with little lids like Chinese hats before her. There would be an uncle or aunt or two to partake of the Friday ritual.

I had the best of it, as I was allowed to go with Olimpia, Nanny's lady's maid, early in the morning to the fish market on Charles Street, which at that time still had cobblestones. Then there would be the long walk back up Beacon Hill almost to the State House with its golden dome, with Olimpia carrying the basket containing the fish and telling me to walk faster or we would be late. I was usually distracted, either gazing at the lovely lavender glass windowpanes in the old brick houses, or being careful not to stub my toes on the uneven brick sidewalks, or, better still, hoping to see a red-coated British soldier or even a cow on the Common.

We always ate this soup with plain Vermont Common Crackers, which we bought out of a barrel. You can purchase them from the Vermont Country Store, Route 100, Weston, Vermont 05161.

1 whole cod or haddock, around 4 pounds
2 cups cold water
2-inch cube of fat salt pork

1½ quarts potatoes, cut into small cubes
1 large onion, sliced
3 garlic cloves, sliced
2 cups boiling water
4 cups milk, scalded
1 teaspoon salt
½ teaspoon pepper
4 tablespoons (½ stick) unsalted butter
Vermont Common Crackers
stick of unsalted butter for crackers

Cut the fish into 2-inch pieces and set aside.

Place the head and tail in a stew pan. Add 2 cups of cold water, bring slowly to a boil, and simmer for 8 minutes.

Cut the salt pork in small bits and render the fat by frying very slowly over low heat. Add the onion and garlic and cook for 5 minutes. Strain the fat into a large pot and add the diced potatoes. Then add the 2 cups of boiling water and cook for 5 minutes.

Add the liquid drained from the head and tail, and the fish pieces, and cover. Simmer for 10 to 12 minutes. Add the milk, salt, pepper, and butter.

Serve the chowder very hot with plain Vermont Common Crackers, buttered and toasted.

Serves 10

Cream of Chicken Soup

This is the perfect soup to serve on cold winter nights in front of a warm, crackling fire.

1 cup fresh milk
2 cups chicken stock
2 tablespoons (¹/₄ stick) unsalted butter
2 tablespoons unbleached flour
salt and pepper to taste
1 farm-fresh egg yolk, at room temperature, slightly beaten
croutons for garnish (page 18)

In a large saucepan, scald the milk. Add the stock and heat through. In a heavy frying pan, melt the butter over low heat, add the flour and seasoning, and stir. Add a bit of the stock to the flour mixture, blend well, and pour back into the stock.

Add some of the warm stock to the bowl with the beaten egg yolk. Stir to blend, then add the egg to the stock in the saucepan.

Serve immediately with homemade croutons.

Serves 4

Soups

BREADS
AND
MUFFINS

White Bread

I used to set the bread bowl on the wood-box next to the stove, a nice draft-free and snug spot. Then one winter's morning I found Miss Purvis fast asleep in the bowl atop the dough with its dishcloth! Pussy had climbed into the bowl of rising dough, thinking it was a warm bed just for her! This is a wonderful bread receipt and makes a large quantity, four loaves — so nice for a large family.

If you make the bread with honey, the crust will be soft instead of crisp. Whole wheat bread is made the same way; use half whole wheat flour and half unbleached white flour and allow just one rising in the bowl. You may also make delicious rolls from the same dough.

2 cups milk
¼ cup (½ stick) unsalted butter
¼ cup sugar or 1 cup honey
2 teaspoons salt
2 cups water
11 cups unbleached flour, approximately
2 packages active dry yeast

¼ cup lukewarm water, 110 degrees F
1 teaspoon sugar or honey

Grease or oil four 5 × 9–inch loaf pans.

In a saucepan, scald the milk, butter, sugar or honey, and salt. Put the mixture in a very large bowl and add the water. Then add 1 cup or so of flour. When the mixture is lukewarm, dissolve the yeast in ¼ cup of water with just a pinch of sugar or honey. Let sit for 5 minutes to proof. When the yeast is foamy, add it to the milk mixture.

Add enough flour to make a nice workable dough and knead for 10 minutes. Place in a very large well-greased bowl, turn once to coat the top, cover with a warm towel, and allow to rise in a warm place for about 1 hour, until double in bulk. When the dough has risen, punch it down and repeat the process.

At the end of the second rising, punch down the dough and divide it into 4 loaves, making sure to smooth out any air bubbles. Place the loaves in the prepared pans, cover them with towels, and allow them to rise until nearly double, about 1 hour.

Preheat the oven to 350 degrees F.

When the dough has almost doubled, bake the loaves in the preheated oven for approximately 1 hour, until they are a crusty brown and sound hollow when tapped. Remove the loaves from the pans and cool them on racks.

Makes 4 loaves

Oatmeal Bread

I won a first prize with a loaf of this bread at the great Danbury Fair when I was fifteen. I assure you I still boast of it at age seventy-seven. It is a truly tasty bread and makes the best bacon, lettuce, and tomato sandwiches. I find that this bread does not freeze well; it is best eaten fresh.

2 cups old-fashioned rolled oats
4 teaspoons salt
1 cup light molasses
2 tablespoons ($^1/_4$ stick) unsalted butter
4 cups boiling water
1 cup lukewarm water, 110 to 115 degrees F
2 packages dry yeast
10 cups unbleached flour

Grease three 5 × 9–inch loaf pans.

Combine the oats, salt, molasses, and butter in a mixing bowl. Add the boiling water and allow to stand for 1 hour.

In a small mixing bowl, measure out 1 cup of lukewarm water. Add to this the yeast and stir to dissolve. Add the cooled oat mixture, along with the flour. Mix lightly, then turn out onto a floured surface and knead well for 8 to 10 minutes, until the dough is smooth and elastic. Place the dough in a large, well-greased mixing bowl, turning the dough over so the top is greased, and cover with a warm towel. Set it in a warm, draft-free place and allow it to rise until doubled, 1 hour or so.

Turn the dough out onto a well-floured surface and divide into 3 sections. Shape into loaves, working out any air bubbles. Place the loaves in the prepared loaf pans, cover, and let rise until doubled, another hour.

Preheat the oven to 350 degrees F.

Bake the loaves in the preheated oven for 1 hour or until they sound hollow when tapped. Remove from pans and cool on racks.

Makes 3 loaves

Bethany's Graham Bread

My oldest daughter, Bethany, is an expert on healthy foods. I do believe that is why she has such glowing success with the many birds she raises. Her Graham Bread is really good and healthful — just ask my flock of bantams, who are always eager for leftover bits of it soaked in goat's milk. This bread freezes well.

3 cups milk
$1/_2$ cup (1 stick) unsalted butter
1 tablespoon salt
$1/_2$ cup light molasses
2 packages dry yeast
$1/_3$ cup lukewarm water, 110 to 115 degrees F
5 cups graham flour
4 cups unbleached flour

Grease two 5 × 9–inch loaf pans.
In a saucepan, scald the milk, allow it to cool slightly, and then add the butter, salt, and molasses. When the mixture is lukewarm, stir the yeast into $1/_3$ of a cup of lukewarm water, stirring to dissolve. Add this to the milk mixture in a large mixing bowl. Stir in the graham flour and beat well. Cover with a warm towel and let the sponge rise until light, 30 minutes to 1 hour.

Stir the sponge down and add the unbleached flour. The dough should be somewhat soft but not sticky. Cover and let rise until doubled, about 1 hour.

Turn the dough out onto a lightly floured surface and divide it in half. Shape into 2 loaves, smoothing out any air bubbles. Place the dough in the loaf pans. Cover and let rise until doubled, 45 minutes to 1 hour.

Preheat the oven to 375 degrees F.

Bake the loaves for 35 to 40 minutes, until they sound hollow when tapped. Remove from pans and cool on racks.

Makes 2 loaves

Rolls for Special Occasions

I invariably make these for Thanksgiving and Christmas dinner. They are particularly good with black raspberry jelly.

The rolls are made in cloverleaf shapes and baked in small individual muffin tins. Their elegant looks will impress your guests. You may want to use half of the dough to make a batch of Butterscotch Rolls (page 30).

2 cups milk

6 tablespoons (^{3}/$_4$ stick) unsalted butter

4 teaspoons sugar

2 teaspoons salt

^{1}/$_4$ cup lukewarm water, 110 degrees F

1 package dry yeast

6 cups unbleached flour

1 large farm-fresh egg, beaten, at room temperature

3 tablespoons unsalted butter, melted

In a medium saucepan, scald the milk. Add the butter, 3 teaspoons of the sugar, and the salt and heat until the mixture is lukewarm (110 degrees F). Pour into a heat-proof bowl.

Measure out ^{1}/$_4$ cup of lukewarm water (110 degrees F) in a glass 1-cup measure. To this add the remaining 1 teaspoon of sugar and the yeast. Stir to dissolve. When the yeast foams, add it to the milk mixture and stir in 3 cups of flour. Beat thoroughly. This makes a sponge that you will now cover and let rise for 30 minutes or so in a warm, draft-free place.

Stir down the sponge when risen. Add the beaten egg and enough flour, 2 ^{1}/$_2$ to 3 cups, to make a soft, workable dough that does not stick to the sides of the bowl. Turn the dough out onto a lightly floured surface and knead it until it is smooth and elastic, 8 to 10 minutes. Place it in a greased bowl, turning it once to coat the top. Cover with a cloth and set in a warm, draft-free spot. Let rise until double, about 1 hour.

Grease 2 muffin tins that each make 1 dozen standard-size muffins.

Punch the dough down and turn it out onto a lightly floured surface. Cut the dough in half, placing one half in the bowl to rest.

To make cloverleaf rolls, pinch off bits of dough about 1 inch in diameter. Roll each bit into a smooth ball with your hands, dip each ball into the melted butter, and place 3 balls in each greased muffin cup. Cover the muffin tins with a cloth and allow the dough to rise until double in size, 30 minutes or so.

Repeat this process with the remainder of the dough.

Preheat the oven to 425 degrees F. Bake the rolls 12 to 15 minutes, until nicely browned.

Makes 2 dozen cloverleaf rolls

Butterscotch Rolls

I make the dough for these rolls in advance and prepare them for breakfast in the morning, served warm from the oven. The house has a wonderful smell while they are baking. They are truly delicious and highly popular with the young; all four of my children doted on them. If you bake them ahead of time, do warm them before serving; it improves the flavor. You can make one batch of the Butterscotch Rolls and one batch of the Rolls for Special Occasions from the basic dough receipt.

1 cup unsalted fresh creamery butter, softened
1 1/2 cups light brown sugar, packed
1 basic dough receipt for Rolls for Special
   Occasions (page 29)
1 cup pecans, chopped
1 cup raisins
3 tablespoons unsalted butter, melted

Grease two 10 × 10 × 2–inch baking dishes.

In a mixing bowl, cream the butter and brown sugar until light. Spread a scant 1/4 portion of the mixture in each of the prepared baking dishes.

Divide the dough into two portions. Roll one half into a rectangle, spread it with 1/4 of the butter and sugar mixture, and sprinkle with half of the chopped pecans and half of the raisins. Roll it up, beginning on the longest side, in jelly-roll fashion, and pinch all of the edges together with your fingers. Cut the roll into sixteen sections, beginning in the center and dividing so as to make equal portions. Place these in the pan, cut side down. Brush the dough with melted butter, then cover and allow to rise until double in size, 30 minutes or so. Immediately work the remainder of the dough in the same manner.

Preheat the oven to 350 degrees F.

Bake the rolls in the preheated oven for 25 to 30 minutes, until nicely browned, taking care not to overbake. Remove from the oven when done. Place a serving platter over the baking dish and invert carefully, allowing the dish to remain on top for a moment so the rolls and topping can settle. Remove the dish with great care, so as not to burn yourself!

Serve warm with fresh creamery butter.

Makes 32 rolls

Hot Cross Buns

I always make a large quantity of these to serve at tea on Good Friday and for breakfast on Easter Sunday. This receipt came from the 1861 edition of *Mrs. Beeton's Book of Household Management*. It was modified at least sixty years ago, to its present delectable state, by my Scottish nanny, Mary Burnett ("Dady"). Absolutely no other hot cross buns can compare. Try them and you will agree. Just be careful not to add the butter when it is too hot, as it will kill the yeast.

Double the receipt if you desire more than twelve buns. I always do, as these have a tendency to disappear when guests or family are about! Also, when I double the receipt I use a total of three packets of yeast for twenty-four buns; the extra yeast makes them lighter.

1 cup milk, warmed to 110 degrees F
1 packet yeast
1/2 cup sugar
2 cups unbleached flour

1/2 teaspoon cinnamon
1 cup currants
1/4 teaspoon salt
1/2 cup (1 stick) unsalted butter, melted and cooled

In a small mixing bowl, stir the milk into the yeast to dissolve, adding 1 teaspoon of the 1/2 cup sugar. In a large bowl, mix together the flour, the remaining sugar, the cinnamon, and the currants. Add the milk and yeast mixture and mix well. Cover with a warm towel, set aside, and allow to rise in a draft-free place for 30 minutes.

Add the salt and melted butter, being sure that the butter is not too hot, so as not to destroy the live yeast. Knead the dough lightly on a generously floured surface, then place in mixing bowl, cover again, and let rise until double in size, 1 hour or so.

Shape the dough into 12 buns and place on a parchment-paper-lined baking sheet. Cover and let rise until double in size, about 30 minutes.

Preheat the oven to 350 degrees F.

Bake the buns in the preheated oven for 15 minutes, until nicely browned. Remove from the oven and cool on racks.

When the buns are cool, make an X on top of each one with a pastry tube filled with a mixture of:

½ cup confectioner's sugar
⅛ teaspoon vanilla extract
2 teaspoons light cream or milk, or enough to make the icing easy to spread

Makes 12 buns

Boston Brown Bread

This receipt came from my grandmother, who may have gotten it from her mother. It is the very thing to serve with Nell's Baked Beans (page 61) on Saturday night. The children called Saturday "Three B's Night," for baked beans, Boston brown bread, and the weekly bath. We had no electricity, so the bath was taken in front of the large kitchen fireplace for warmth. First, blankets were hung to make a draftless enclosure, then out came the tub, a large copper kettle filled with boiling water (the same kettle that sits on my stove to this day), two pails of cold water, soap, a towel, and a sponge. It was a delightful event, though a bit chilly in winter, when the side facing the fire would be very hot and water would freeze on the floor on the opposite side.

Then as now, Boston brown bread was made in a pudding tin and steamed for three hours. It has an irresistible smell.

1 cup unbleached flour
1 cup graham flour
1 cup yellow cornmeal
1/2 cup sugar
1 1/2 teaspoons salt
1 teaspoon baking soda
1/2 cup light molasses
1 1/2 cups sour milk or buttermilk

2 tablespoons (1/4 stick) unsalted butter, melted
3/4 cup dark raisins

Generously butter a pudding mold, melon mold, or two one-pound coffee cans. You can use aluminum foil or wax paper to cover the tin.

In a large mixing bowl, combine the flours, cornmeal, sugar, and salt. Mix the baking soda with the molasses and add them along with the milk to the dry ingredients. Add the butter and raisins and stir well.

Pour the batter into a well-buttered mold. It should never be filled more than three-quarters full. The cover should be buttered before being placed on the mold, and then tied down with string; otherwise the rising of the bread may force the cover off.

For steaming, place the mold on a trivet in a kettle of boiling water, allowing the water to come halfway up the sides of the mold. Reduce the heat to a simmer, cover the kettle, and steam for 3 hours, adding more boiling water as needed.

Makes 2 loaves, using one-pound coffee cans

Baking-Powder Biscuits

I serve these hot from the oven with fresh creamery butter and homemade raspberry preserves that I have bottled myself from my own raspberry patch. Occasionally I like to add a grated sharp cheese, such as a Vermont cheddar, to the dough as I mix it together. These are marvelous served with my Corgi Cottage Soup (page 13).

1 farm-fresh egg, at room temperature
1/2 to 3/4 cup milk
2 cups unbleached flour
4 teaspoons baking powder
1/2 teaspoon salt
1/3 cup shortening

Preheat the oven to 475 degrees F and grease a cookie sheet.

Crack the egg into a 1-cup glass measure. Mix well with a fork. Add milk to the 3/4-cup mark and mix well again.

In a large mixing bowl, sift the flour, baking powder, and salt. Lightly mix in the shortening with your fingers. Stir in the milk mixture, taking care not to overwork the dough. On a lightly floured surface, roll or pat the dough to 1/2-inch thickness and cut with a 2 1/4-inch floured biscuit cutter. Place the rounds 1 inch apart on the prepared baking sheet.

Bake the biscuits in the preheated oven for 10 to 12 minutes, until nicely browned.

Makes approximately 18 small biscuits

The Tasha Tudor Cookbook

Date and Nut Bread

This bread is delicious sliced very thin and spread with cream cheese. Serve these sandwiches for tea.

1 cup dates, chopped
¹/₂ cup sugar
³/₄ cup boiling water
¹/₄ cup (¹/₂ stick) unsalted butter, softened
1 farm-fresh egg, well beaten
1 teaspoon baking soda

1³/₄ cups unbleached flour
¹/₂ teaspoon salt
¹/₂ cup English walnuts, chopped

Grease well one 4 ¹/₂ × 9–inch loaf pan or two 3 × 6–inch pans.

In a large mixing bowl, combine the dates, sugar, and boiling water. Mix well and allow to cool.

Preheat the oven to 350 degrees F.

When the mixture has cooled, stir in the remaining ingredients. Pour the batter into the prepared bread tin.

Bake in the preheated oven for 40 to 50 minutes (less for smaller loaves) or until done when tested with a toothpick.

Remove the bread from the oven, take it out of the pan, and place it on a rack to cool completely.

Makes 1 large loaf or 2 smaller loaves

Great-Grandmother Tudor's Cornbread

This is a very old family receipt. It came from my great-great-grandfather Colonel William Tudor's wife, Delia, who I am ashamed to say was a Tory before she married him. Children love the cornbread split and buttered and spread with warm maple syrup or raspberry jam. It is best made in a heavy cast-iron pan that makes twelve individual pieces; any pan will work, but iron imparts a unique crustiness.

1/2 cup (1 stick) unsalted butter, softened
2/3 cup sugar
2 farm-fresh eggs, at room temperature, separated
1 cup unbleached flour
3 teaspoons baking powder
1/4 teaspoon salt
1 cup milk, lukewarm
1 cup yellow cornmeal

Preheat the oven to 400 degrees F. Grease an iron cornbread pan that makes 12 sticks, or a muffin tin, with peanut oil.

In a large mixing bowl, cream the butter and sugar and add the egg yolks, slightly beaten. Stir well. In another bowl, beat the egg whites until stiff peaks form. Sift the flour with the baking powder and salt, then add it alternately with the milk to the creamed butter. Stir in the cornmeal, then fold in the beaten egg whites.

Pour the batter into the prepared pan.

Bake in the preheated oven for 25 minutes, until beautifully browned.

Makes 12 servings

Robie's Blueberry Muffins

There is nothing finer than blueberry muffins served hot from the wood cook-stove. Small wild berries are the best kind to use in this receipt.

I learned how to make these muffins from Robie Mock, a neighbor of ours in Webster, New Hampshire. She was a real character and so good to my children. They all loved her. She even put up with Tweedy, our tame starling, who was enthralled by her hairdo. He would fly to her head and poke at her permanent wave, talking and fluttering in sheer delight. Kind Robie never minded.

We would make her muffins for church suppers and deliver them in our buggy, drawn by Rebecca, our dun-colored mare. It was an event to drive to the supper with children and corgi dogs in back, and two or three tins of Robie's blueberry muffins. The wood thrushes would be singing as the sun set. It is a happy remembrance.

½ cup shortening
1 cup sugar
2 farm-fresh eggs, at room temperature
2¼ cups unbleached flour, divided
¼ teaspoon salt
3 teaspoons baking powder
¾ cup fresh dairy milk
1 teaspoon vanilla extract
1 cup blueberries, fresh or frozen, not thawed
sugar and cinnamon for topping

Preheat the oven to 400 degrees F. Line muffin tins with paper baking cups.

In a large mixing bowl, cream the shortening and sugar together. Add the eggs and beat the mixture well. Sift 2 cups of the flour with the salt and baking powder and add it to the bowl, alternating with the milk. Beat the mixture just until smooth, then add the vanilla. Mix the remaining ¼ cup flour with the berries, just enough to coat them. Gently fold these into the mixture.

Fill the prepared tins about ⅔ full. Sprinkle each muffin lightly with sugar and cinnamon.

Bake in the preheated oven for 20 to 25 minutes, until lightly browned.

Makes 18 muffins

Waffles or Pancakes

Pancakes were a winter favorite with my children. Served with *real* maple syrup, they are heavenly. And made on the wood stove on a heavy iron griddle, they are really a treat for breakfast or supper. There was the added fun of feeding the first-cooked to the hens — "hen pancakes," they were called.

We once had a Jersey cow who devoured waffles. A look of bliss would come to her liquid brown eyes as she munched. The children claimed that her milk always tasted better on Sunday nights for this reason.

1 1/2 cups unbleached flour
3 teaspoons baking powder
1/2 teaspoon salt
2 teaspoons sugar
2 farm-fresh eggs, at room temperature
1 1/4 cups milk
3 tablespoons unsalted butter, melted

Sift into a bowl the flour, baking powder, salt, and sugar. Beat the eggs lightly in a second mixing bowl. Stir in the milk and the melted butter. Add the egg mixture to the dry ingredients and blend.

To make pancakes, spoon the batter onto a hot, greased griddle or skillet. When the tops are bubbly, turn them and cook the other side until nicely brown. Place the pancakes on warm plates and serve immediately.

To make waffles, spoon the batter into a preheated waffle iron. The waffles will be cooked when steam no longer rises from the waffle iron. Serve immediately on warm plates.

Makes 14 4-inch pancakes or 6 waffles

Blueberry Coffee Cake

This is very tasty served warm from the oven for breakfast.

$3/4$ cup sugar
$1/4$ cup shortening
1 farm-fresh egg, at room temperature
$1/2$ cup milk
2 cups unbleached flour
2 teaspoons baking powder
1 teaspoon salt
2 cups blueberries, fresh or frozen, not thawed

Topping:
$1/2$ cup sugar
$1/3$ cup unbleached flour, sifted
$1/2$ teaspoon cinnamon
$1/4$ cup ($1/2$ stick) unsalted butter, softened
$1/2$ cup pecans, chopped (optional)

Preheat the oven to 375 degrees F. Grease and flour a 9 × 9 × 2–inch square cake tin.

In a mixing bowl, cream together the sugar and the shortening. Stir in the egg and then the milk. Sift in the flour, baking powder, and salt and mix quickly. Then carefully fold in the blueberries.

Spread the batter in the prepared pan. Combine all of the topping ingredients and sprinkle the mixture over the batter. Bake in the preheated oven for 45 to 50 minutes. Cut in squares and serve warm with butter.

Serves 9

Josephine Knapper's Bran Muffins

This receipt was given to me years ago by a friend who had in turn been given it by another dear friend, Josephine Knapper. It is a wonderfully easy receipt that you will want to share with family and friends. It makes a large quantity — enough for six dozen or so muffins — and keeps well in the refrigerator for up to six weeks. I keep it in a crock with a lid on it and place it in the dairy cooler. It is just the thing to have on hand for unexpected guests who happen to pay a call, as the muffins can be baking in the oven while you put the kettle on for tea.

2 cups Nabisco 100 percent bran
2 cups boiling water
2 1/2 cups sugar
1 cup vegetable oil
4 farm-fresh eggs, at room temperature
4 cups Kellogg's All Bran or other 100 percent
*   bran cereal*
5 cups unbleached flour
1 1/2 teaspoons salt
5 teaspoons baking soda
1 quart buttermilk
1 pound dark raisins

Preheat the oven to 400 degrees F. Grease muffin tins with shortening, or line them with baking cups.

Place the Nabisco bran in a medium mixing bowl and cover with 2 cups of boiling water. Stir and set aside to cool.

In a large mixing bowl, combine the sugar and the oil. Add the eggs and All Bran and stir. Sift in the flour, salt, and baking soda, alternating with the buttermilk. After you have mixed the batter well, stir in the cooled bran mixture and the raisins.

Fill the prepared muffin tins 2/3 full and bake in the preheated oven for 15 to 20 minutes.

When the muffins are done, remove them from the oven and allow them to cool in the tins on a rack for 10 minutes or so.

Store any remaining batter in an airtight covered container and keep it refrigerated. *Do not stir the batter when you spoon it out to make the muffins; simply dip it out from the top.*

Makes 6 dozen muffins

MAIN DISHES

Roast of Beef

This is a once-a-year treat, as New Year's is the only time we cook a roast of beef. I always make Yorkshire Pudding (receipt follows) to accompany the standing rib roast.

4-pound standing rib roast
2 cloves garlic, peeled and pressed
salt and pepper

Preheat the oven to 325 degrees F.

Place the meat on a rack in a shallow roasting pan, fat side up. Rub the meat with the pressed garlic, salt, and pepper.

If you have a meat thermometer, insert it in the thickest section of the beef and as near the center as possible, so as not to touch fat or bone.

Place the roasting pan, uncovered, in the center of the preheated oven. The cooking time will depend upon how well done you prefer your meat. A general cooking guide follows:

Doneness	Cooking Time	Meat Thermometer Reading
Rare	22–26 minutes per pound	140 degrees
Medium	26–30 minutes per pound	160 degrees
Well Done	33–35 minutes per pound	170 degrees

When the roast is done, remove it from the oven and allow it to stand for a while to soak up the juices.

Serves 12

Yorkshire Pudding

This is a must with the New Year's roast beef. Make the pudding in the roasting pan after the roast is done and has been removed to rest before carving. Don't drain the pan; cook it right in the drippings. I can feel cholesterol-intimidated people squirming in horror. However, once a year will not hurt you, and life is too short not to enjoy a few treats.

My Scottish nanny, Dady, taught me how to make this beloved British dish. Once, when crossing a street in Brattleboro, I was stopped by a youth who said, "I hear you make the best Yorkshire pudding of anybody around." Dady taught me well.

1 cup unbleached flour
$^1/_4$ teaspoon salt
1 cup milk
2 farm-fresh eggs

Preheat the oven to 450 degrees F.

In a bowl, mix together the flour and salt, then gradually add the milk to make a smooth paste. Stir in the eggs and beat 2 minutes with an egg beater.

Pour the batter into the pan that the roast beef was cooked in and bake for 20 to 30 minutes. Cut the pudding into squares and serve immediately.

Serves 8 to 10

Bethany's Braised Beef

This receipt is just the thing for a winter's meal. It cooks best, of course, on a wood stove, mingling its tempting smell with wood smoke. However, it can easily be made over anything that heats, even an open fire.

My daughter Bethany found the receipt years ago in some now-forgotten cookery book. She is credited as the rediscoverer of this satisfying meal. Serve it with horseradish, which complements most beef dishes.

1 tablespoon peanut oil or shortening
unbleached flour to coat meat
salt and pepper to taste
3 pounds beef, top or bottom round
2 thin slices salt pork
1/2 teaspoon each fresh-chopped thyme, basil, and summer savory
1 or 2 bay leaves
1/2 teaspoon peppercorns
1 cup onions (2 medium), sliced
2 cloves garlic, peeled
3 cups boiling water
1 cup carrot, peeled and cut in 3-inch pieces
1 cup turnip, peeled and diced
3 ribs celery (with leaves), cut in 3-inch pieces
6 small potatoes, scrubbed
2 tablespoons unbleached flour

Preheat the oven to 250 degrees F.

In a deep, cast-iron baking dish, heat the peanut oil or shortening over a medium flame. Flour, salt, and pepper the meat, place it in the baking dish, and add the salt pork. Brown the meat slowly and thoroughly on all sides, taking care not to pierce it with the fork when turning.

Season the meat with the herbs and peppercorns, place the onions and garlic on top, and pour 3 cups of boiling water into the pot. Cover tightly and roast in the oven for 4 hours, turning the meat occasionally. Throughout the cooking, the liquid should be kept below the boiling point.

When the meat is nearly done, place the vegetables around it and return the pot to the oven for an additional 40 minutes or so, until both the vegetables and the meat are tender.

Thicken the liquid by blending two tablespoons of flour with a little cold water in a small mixing bowl. Add a little hot liquid from the roast and then return the mixture to the pot.

Serves 6 or more

Leg of Lamb

This dish needs a long slow roasting to be truly good. It is best served with Oven-Browned Potatoes (receipt follows), peas fresh from the garden, and homemade Mint Sauce (page 66).

6-pound leg of lamb
6 cloves garlic, peeled
1 small onion, cut in half
2 teaspoons rosemary leaves
salt and pepper

Preheat the oven to 325 degrees F.

Place the leg of lamb in a shallow roasting pan. Pierce the fat portion in several places and insert a clove of garlic in each slit. Rub the meat all over with the onion, then sprinkle it generously with rosemary and finally with salt and pepper.

Place the pan in the preheated oven and roast the lamb for approximately 3 to 3½ hours, until a meat thermometer registers 175–182 degrees F, depending on the doneness you desire. After removing the leg of lamb from the oven, allow it to stand for several minutes before carving, just as you would any roast, to allow the juices to be drawn back into the meat.

Serve the lamb on well-warmed plates.

Serves 12 or more

Oven-Browned Potatoes

Oven-browned potatoes are to roast leg of lamb what a puddle is to a duck. I always parboil them for a few minutes before placing them in the pan with the partially cooked roast. They should be rolled in the drippings when added to the pan, and turned once or twice during roasting so they will be nicely browned all over.

12 medium-size, firm potatoes

Peel the potatoes, placing them in a pan of cold water as you finish peeling them, to keep them from turning brown. Boil the pared potatoes for 10 minutes, drain off the water, and place the potatoes in the pan with the roast leg of lamb during the final 30 minutes of cooking time. Turn them occasionally to brown evenly.

Serves 12

Beef Stew

This is a good standby that makes use of the less expensive cuts of beef. Most any cookbook includes the basic receipt, but use your imagination and add plenty of onions, garlic, and fresh herbs. Add the potatoes last, as they take less time to cook than the other vegetables. This stew makes a meal in itself when served with a crisp green salad and Cornbread (page 360) or spooned over split and buttered Baking-Powder Biscuits (page 34).

2 pounds beef, bottom round, cut in 2-inch
    pieces
unbleached flour seasoned with salt and pepper
    to coat meat
1 tablespoon shortening
1 quart boiling water
4 cloves garlic, peeled and finely sliced
$^1/_2$ cup yellow onion, chopped
1 small green pepper, diced
1 cup celery, sliced
2 cups potatoes, peeled and diced
1 cup turnips, peeled and diced
2 cups carrots, peeled and diced
$^1/_2$ cup parsnips, peeled and diced

2 Knorr's beef bouillon cubes
$^1/_2$ teaspoon each fresh thyme and parsley,
    chopped
1 or 2 bay leaves
1 tablespoon unbleached flour

Dredge the beef chunks in the seasoned flour and sear them in melted shortening in a heavy pot. Pour 1 quart of boiling water over the meat, then add the garlic. Cover and simmer for 2 hours, adding more water as needed.

Add the vegetables, bouillon cubes, and herbs, and season to taste. Simmer an additional 30 to 60 minutes until the vegetables are tender, adding more water if necessary. Thicken the sauce with a bit of flour, 1 tablespoon or so, by adding some of the gravy to the flour and then stirring the thickener into the pot. Simmer for a few more minutes before serving.

Serves 8

Meat Loaf

I serve this dish with tender, buttery noodles and a rich gravy made from the meat drippings as the meat loaf bakes. A green vegetable and a good bread round out the meal nicely.

3/4 pound ground beef
1/4 pound ground pork
1 egg yolk, beaten
2 tablespoons fresh parsley, chopped
1 tablespoon unsalted butter, softened
1 tablespoon soft bread crumbs
1 teaspoon lemon juice, freshly squeezed
1 teaspoon salt
1/4 teaspoon freshly ground pepper
1 teaspoon onion, finely minced

For Basting:
1/4 cup (1/2 stick) unsalted butter, melted
1 cup vegetable or beef stock (or Knorr's beef bouillon, if homemade stock is not on hand)

For Gravy:
1 tablespoon unbleached flour

Preheat the oven to 350 degrees F.

In a mixing bowl, combine the meat-loaf ingredients with your hands. Transfer the mixture to a lightly buttered, shallow baking dish and shape it into a loaf. Pour the stock and butter for basting over the loaf.

Bake for approximately 1 hour in the preheated oven, basting as often as possible.

When the meat loaf is done, remove it to a warmed serving platter and keep it warm in the oven while you prepare gravy from the drippings.

To make the gravy, pour the juices from the meat into a small saucepan. Put 1 tablespoon of flour in a small mixing bowl and add a tablespoon or so of the juices, stirring to blend. When the mixture is smooth, stir in a bit more of the juices, then add this thickener to the drippings in the saucepan. Stir over medium heat until the gravy is thickened and smooth.

Serves 4 to 6

Turkey Roasted in the Tin Kitchen

You have to have a fireplace for this receipt, as well as a tin kitchen, also known as a reflector oven. To my mind it is the *only* way to cook a fresh turkey.

Roasting the mighty bird in this fashion takes less time than baking one in a regular oven — and oh, the difference in taste!

Stuffing:
2¹/₂ cups
  chicken
  stock
¹/₂ cup (1
  stick)
  unsalted butter
16-ounce package
  Pepperidge Farm herb-
  seasoned stuffing
1 large onion, finely chopped
4 ribs celery, chopped
6 cloves garlic, minced
1 cup fresh mixed herbs: parsley, thyme,
  savory, sage, and marjoram, finely
  chopped

20-pound turkey
bacon drippings
salt and pepper

In a saucepan, bring the chicken stock and the butter to a boil. Remove from the heat.

Place the stuffing and other ingredients in a large mixing bowl. Pour the stock and butter over all and toss lightly to mix.

Stuff the bird, rub it well with bacon drippings, and salt and pepper it lightly. Truss it carefully and insert the spit, making sure to secure the bird with skewers and twine to keep it from sliding off the spit. Place the spit before a fire of hard wood, turning it every so often to cook the turkey evenly. Barricade the bird from corgies and cats with a firescreen. Baste it as often as you can with the drippings, collected in a pipkin or small bowl placed by the tin kitchen's spout. If you start your bird by nine in the morning, you will have him roasted to a nicety for a two o'clock dinner.

To serve, remove the turkey from the tin kitchen, detach the skewers and spit, and place it on your best and largest platter.

Simply unsurpassed!

Serves approximately 20

Roast Chicken

This is a particular specialty of mine. You must obtain a farm-raised chicken for good flavor — a *roaster*, not a fryer. You may stuff it if you are so inclined, but I do not bother. Instead, I always make a good quantity of Mashed Potatoes (page 62) to accompany it. A bit of currant jelly makes a good complement if you happen to have some on hand, as do vegetables from the garden.

1 farm-raised roasting chicken, approxi-
    mately 6 pounds
salt and pepper
butter or cold bacon drippings
4 large cloves garlic, peeled
1 large onion, peeled
2 fresh bay leaves
1 large handful of assorted fresh herbs,
    especially tarragon and sage

Preheat the oven to 350 degrees F. Wash the chicken and pat it dry. Place it in a roasting pan, salt and pepper it, and rub it with butter or cold bacon drippings. Insert 2 large cloves of garlic by piercing a hole beside each drum-stick. Place another garlic clove in both front and back cavities. Put the onion in the back cavity along with the bay leaves and the fresh herbs. Truss with string, place in the preheated oven, and cook for 2 hours, basting frequently.

Serves 4 to 6

Chicken Croquettes

This is a good way to stretch leftover chicken. Meat or fish croquettes are equally delicious. Just be especially careful when cooking with deep fat, as it can spatter. If you make tiny versions of these, you can serve them on toothpicks as appetizers with ketchup.

4 tablespoons (¹/₂ stick) unsalted butter
¹/₃ cup unbleached flour
¹/₈ teaspoon fresh thyme, minced
2 tablespoons fresh parsley, minced
¹/₄ teaspoon salt
¹/₈ teaspoon pepper
1 tablespoon onion, minced
1 small clove garlic, minced
1 cup milk
¹/₂ cube Knorr's chicken bouillon, crumbled
2¹/₂ to 3 cups ground cooked chicken
1 large farm-fresh egg
2 tablespoons water
²/₃ cup Ritz crackers, crushed
vegetable oil for frying

In a heavy iron frying pan, melt the butter, then add the flour mixed with the seasonings, onion, and garlic. Stir until well blended. Pour the milk into the pan while stirring constantly. Bring the mixture to a boil, then lower the heat and simmer for 2 minutes until the sauce thickens and bubbles. Taste, and if the sauce is lacking flavor at this point, add just a small piece of Knorr's chicken bouillon, stirring to dissolve it. The sauce will be very thick.

Add the sauce to the ground chicken, mix, and then chill thoroughly so the mixture will be easy to handle.

Mix the egg and water with a fork in a pie plate.

Divide the chilled chicken mixture into 10 or 12 little log-shaped portions. Dip each log into crushed Ritz crackers, then into the egg mixture, and finally into the Ritz crackers again, taking care that all of the sides are covered generously to keep the logs from bursting while cooking.

Fry the croquettes in deep fat at 365 degrees until golden brown, approximately 3 minutes. Watch the thermometer and do not allow the temperature to rise above 365 degrees. Cook only 3 or 4 croquettes at a time so that the hot oil does not boil over. *And above all, do not leave it unattended even for a moment!* As you finish cooking the croquettes, drain them on brown paper bags or paper toweling and place them in the oven to keep them warm.

Serves 4

Salmon

The Fourth of July calls for salmon with peas picked fresh from the garden, but getting home-grown peas to ripen in Vermont for this great occasion is a real challenge. Along with freshly dug tiny new potatoes, this is an annual treat.

2 1½-inch salmon steaks
1 tablespoon unsalted butter
salt and pepper to taste
Parsley Butter (receipt follows)

Preheat the oven to 400 degrees F.
Place the steaks on a buttered baking dish, salt and pepper them lightly, and place a teaspoon of butter atop each one. Bake them for about 25 minutes in the preheated oven. If you prefer to broil the fish, preheat the broiler and place the steaks on a rack in the broiler pan. Watch them carefully, and do not overcook.
Serve hot from the oven with Parsley Butter.

Serves 4

Parsley Butter

¼ cup (½ stick) unsalted butter
½ tablespoon fresh parsley, chopped
½ teaspoon salt
⅛ teaspoon pepper
2–3 sprigs fresh parsley
¾ tablespoon lemon juice, freshly squeezed

In a mixing bowl, work the butter until it is soft and creamy. Stir in the salt, pepper, and parsley, then the lemon juice, very slowly. Form the butter into a mound and place it on a serving dish, adorned with sprigs of fresh parsley.

Prickly Fish Balls

You can purchase salt cod in a little wooden box in a good fish market or grocery store. Codfish balls fried in deep fat have tiny "tiggy winkle" spines. They are *the* dish for Easter breakfast. Saving certain dishes for certain occasions makes them taste particularly delicious. In my youth there was a season for all things; today people miss the delight of having strawberries only in season. Shakespeare put it best in *Love's Labour's Lost:*

> At Christmas I no more desire a rose
> Than wish a snow in May's newfangled
>   mirth;
> But like of each thing that in season
>   grows.

1 cup salt cod
2¹/₂ cups diced potatoes
¹/₂ tablespoon unsalted butter
1 farm-fresh egg, well beaten
¹/₈ teaspoon pepper

Freshen the salt cod by placing it in a bowl of cold water overnight. The flesh side should be down so that the salt can sink to the bottom when it is extracted.

Once the fish has been freshened, pick it into very small pieces or cut it with scissors.

Wash and pare the potatoes and then soak them in water, cutting them into cubes before measuring them.

Cook the fish and the potatoes in boiling water until the potatoes are tender. Drain them thoroughly in a colander, then return them to the kettle in which they were cooked and shake them over the heat until they are thoroughly dry. Remove them from the heat and mash them carefully, being sure there are no lumps. Add the butter, egg, and pepper. Beat with a fork for a minute.

Take the mixture up by spoonfuls and fry it in deep fat heated to 385 degrees F, allowing 6 fish balls for each batch. When they are done, drain them on brown paper. Reheat the fat after each batch before repeating the process.

Serve with a good ketchup.

Serves 4

Cheese Soufflé

This is an excellent dish when unexpected guests arrive and you want to ask them for lunch. All you need to add is a green garden salad and some good bread. Be sure everyone is seated at the table as soon as the soufflé is ready, for it falls almost immediately. A soufflé is easy to make and elegant to serve — but do use really fresh eggs.

1 cup milk
1 cup soft white homemade or Pepperidge
*   Farm bread crumbs*
1 cup Vermont sharp cheddar cheese, diced
1 tablespoon unsalted butter
¹/₂ teaspoon salt
3 farm-fresh eggs, separated

Preheat the oven to 350 degrees F and butter a 1 ¹/₂-quart soufflé dish.

In a saucepan, scald the milk. Place the bread crumbs, cheese, butter, and salt in a mixing bowl and pour the milk over all. Then add the well-beaten egg yolks, stir well, and fold in the stiffly beaten egg whites.

Pour into the prepared baking dish. Place in preheated oven and bake for 20 minutes until puffed and golden brown.

Serve immediately!

Serves 4

ACCOMPANIMENTS

Baked Beans

These I learned to make from Nell Dorr, the well-known children's photographer. No one, to my mind, has exceeded the art of Nell and her Rolleiflex camera. No posing, no flashes, just pure magic.

Nell Dorr gave memorable supper parties in her home, the West Branch, in Westport, Connecticut. I recall the many artists who attended these agreeable gatherings; Robert Lawson was one. It was all delightfully informal, with small tables set about the four small rooms. Nell looked lovely, as she always did, in her long frocks, with Queen Anne's lace in her dark hair.

Her famous baked beans and homemade bread were always served, and no other baked beans can compare.

2 cups (1 pound) pea beans
pinch baking soda
2 medium onions, peeled
1 slice bacon
2 tablespoons light molasses
1 quart tomato juice
salt and pepper to taste
1 tablespoon dark brown sugar, divided
1/2 pound good sausage meat
1/2 teaspoon Colman's dry English mustard

Wash and pick over the beans, then parboil them until their skin pops when you blow on them. Drain, cover with fresh water, add a pinch of baking soda, and simmer until the beans squash when you pinch them. Drain.

Now put the onions in the bottom of a bean pot, add half the beans and the slice of bacon, the molasses, 1 cup of the tomato juice, and salt and pepper. Sprinkle with two teaspoons of the brown sugar. Layer the rest of the beans with sausage meat, English mustard, and the remainder of the brown sugar. Fill the pot with tomato juice to cover the beans.

Preheat the oven to 250 degrees F.

Cover the beans and bake them all day in a slow oven. About halfway through baking, taste for seasoning. Be careful not to overdo the brown sugar. Stir the beans 2 or 3 times during baking. If the liquid boils away, just add more tomato juice, making sure to keep the beans covered during baking. Bake for about 8 hours or until the beans are tender.

Serves 10 to 12

Mashed Potatoes

The secret of these is a good old-fashioned potato ricer, along with plenty of milk, butter, salt, pepper, and a goodly chunk of cream cheese. They *must* be served *hot*. They can be kept warm over a pot of boiling water while you prepare other vegetables. The leftovers make delicious potato cakes sautéed in butter. You must use good fresh potatoes; your own garden-grown ones are the best. I raise Green Mountains, whose flavor is unsurpassed. One can always be sure spring is on the way when the potatoes start to sprout.

4 medium potatoes
salt and pepper to taste
1/4 cup milk
4 tablespoons (1/2 stick) unsalted butter
4 tablespoons cream cheese

Peel and wash the potatoes and place them in a medium-size pan. Add enough water just to cover them, and a small quantity of salt. Place the pan over medium-high heat until the water begins to boil, then lower the heat to medium to keep the water at a gentle boil. Cook the potatoes for 20 minutes or so, until they are fork-tender.

In a small saucepan, warm the milk, butter, and cream cheese.

When the potatoes are done, drain off the water and put them through a ricer or mash them in the same pot. Add the warm milk mixture and whip the potatoes with a wooden spoon until they are light and fluffy. Salt and pepper to taste.

Serves 4

Macaroni and Cheese

Macaroni and cheese was a favorite dish of Thomas Jefferson. This is our family receipt and the one that we use for our summer Stillwater Parties, as it can be made in large quantities and is always popular. It is particularly good when served with a fine smoked ham. I feel certain Mr. Jefferson would have enjoyed it.

2 cups (7 ounces) elbow macaroni
5 tablespoons unsalted butter
1/4 cup unbleached flour
2 cups milk
1 cup (4 ounces) Vermont sharp cheddar
*   cheese, grated*
salt and pepper
4 ounces Velveeta, cubed
1/2 cup crumbled Ritz crackers for topping

Preheat the oven to 350 degrees F and butter a shallow 1 1/2-quart baking dish.

Cook the macaroni in boiling salted water until just tender. Drain it while you prepare the cream sauce.

In a large saucepan, melt 4 tablespoons of the butter, then whisk in the flour and add the milk. Stir the mixture until it thickens, then add the cheddar cheese and stir it in until it melts. Season with salt and pepper. Cut the Velveeta into 1/2-inch chunks and stir it into the white sauce, but *do not* allow it to melt completely. Place the drained macaroni in the prepared baking dish, pour the cheese sauce over it, and stir gently to mix. Sprinkle the crumbled Ritz crackers generously over the top and dot with the remaining butter.

Bake in the preheated oven for 20 to 25 minutes, until browned and bubbly.

Serves 4 to 6

Cranberry Sauce

This receipt is from my father's side of the family, who originally settled on Cape Cod. At Thanksgiving and Christmas I use fresh-picked cranberries to make this delicious sauce. After I have cooked the sauce, I pour it into my great-grandmother's mold, which is made of pottery and has an indented form in the pattern of an ear of corn. It turns out beautifully if one is careful when unmolding it. I feel at that time like Mrs. Bob Cratchit, in the trying moment of "turning out the pudding."

2 pounds fresh-picked cranberries, washed and picked over
2 cups cold water, approximately
2 pounds sugar

Place the cranberries in a large saucepan and add enough cold water to not quite cover the berries when they are pressed down. Add the sugar. Bring to a simmer and skim off the foam occasionally. Cook the cranberries until their juice jells when it is dropped on a cold plate. Pour into a mold and chill overnight.

To remove the sauce from the mold, gently run a paring knife around the edge, dip the mold in hot water for a moment, and then invert it onto a platter to serve.

Yields approximately 1 1/2 quarts

Mint Sauce

Mint sauce is another family favorite that has been made for generations. I serve it with all of my lamb dishes. This sauce will keep for years and improves with age. Be sure to use only true spearmint, as other mints are not as tasty.

This receipt yields only one cup of sauce. To make larger amounts for Christmas gifts, just increase the quantities, keeping the same proportions.

1/2 cup sugar
1/2 cup cider vinegar
1/2 cup finely chopped fresh spearmint leaves

Place the sugar and cider vinegar in a saucepan, mix them together, and simmer for 20 minutes.

While the mixture is still hot, add the chopped spearmint leaves. Pour this into a glass canning jar, cover tightly, and shake well.

Makes 1 cup

DESSERTS
AND
BEVERAGES

Chocolate Cake

My mother was an excellent cook and a gracious hostess. This is her receipt. I learned much about the art of entertaining from her.

This cake is very tasty frosted with Boiled White Frosting (page 73) or, as a dieter's downfall, with Seth's Fudge (page 86). You can also make cupcakes with this receipt, but be certain to shorten the baking time slightly so they do not become dry. The cupcakes are delicious frosted with Cocoa Frosting (receipt follows).

3 squares Baker's unsweetened baking chocolate
1 cup plus 4 tablespoons sugar
²/₃ cup plus 2 tablespoons milk
6 tablespoons (³/₄ stick) unsalted butter, at room temperature
1 cup sugar
2 farm-fresh eggs, at room temperature, separated
1¹/₂ cups cake flour
3 teaspoons baking powder
¹/₂ teaspoon salt
1 teaspoon vanilla extract

Preheat the oven to 350 degrees F. Grease and flour two 9-inch round cake tins, cut rounds of waxed paper for the bottoms, and grease and flour them.

Combine in a double boiler, over hot water, the chocolate, 4 tablespoons of the sugar, and 2 tablespoons of the milk.

In a large mixing bowl, cream the butter, then add the rest of the sugar, the beaten egg yolks, and the melted chocolate mixture. Stir well. Sift together the dry ingredients and add them to the batter, alternating with the rest of the milk. Fold in the stiffly beaten egg whites and the vanilla.

Pour the batter into the prepared tins.

Bake in the preheated oven for 20 minutes, or until the cake begins to pull away from the sides of the tin. Check for doneness with a cake tester, taking care not to overbake, so the cakes do not become dry. Remove the cakes from the oven, place them on racks to cool in their tins for 10 minutes, then remove them from the tins, peel off the waxed paper, and cool them completely on racks. Frost when the cakes are cool.

Makes 1 cake or 24 cupcakes, to serve 10 or more

Cocoa Frosting

This Cocoa Frosting is perfection on my Chocolate Cake (receipt above). When the children were little, I used to make cupcakes from the cake receipt and take them along on picnics.

2 cups confectioner's sugar
4 tablespoons cocoa
4 tablespoons ($^1/_2$ stick) unsalted butter, melted
4 tablespoons strong hot coffee
1 teaspoon vanilla extract

Sift the powdered sugar and cocoa into a medium-size mixing bowl. Add the melted butter and enough coffee to make a good spreading consistency, then beat well with an old-fashioned egg beater. Stir in the vanilla.

Spread the frosting on cooled cakes.

Yields 2 cups, enough to frost an 8- or 9-inch double layer cake or 24 cupcakes

Becky's Birthday Cake

This receipt has been the family birthday cake for as long as I can remember. For many of my daughter Bethany's birthday parties we placed the cake on a wood-shingle raft, surrounded it with flowers, and floated it down our stream. We also had a shingle raft and a candle for each child's sandwich. We positioned the guests downstream, and when the right moment came we would light the candles and send the cake and its flotilla of shingle boats out into the stream. It was dark by then, so you can imagine the surprise of the guests at the sudden appearance of this fairy convoy. Once, the cake took off into a faster current and my son Seth had to wade in to rescue it.

If you wish to know more details, I suggest you obtain a copy of my book *Becky's Birthday* from the Jenny Wren Press. I believe you will enjoy the story, which is entirely true.

I traditionally ice this cake with Boiled White Frosting (receipt follows) tinted pink.

1 farm-fresh egg, at room temperature, separated
4 tablespoons (¹/₂ stick) unsalted butter, softened
³/₄ cup sugar
1 ¹/₂ cups cake flour, sifted

2 teaspoons baking powder
¹/₈ teaspoon salt
¹/₂ cup milk
¹/₂ teaspoon vanilla extract

Preheat the oven to 350 degrees F. Grease and flour 2 8-inch round cake tins, cut rounds of waxed paper to fit the bottoms, and grease and flour the paper.

Beat the egg yolk in a small bowl.

In a large mixing bowl, cream butter and sugar well, then add the well-beaten yolk. Sift together the dry ingredients and add them to the mixture, alternating with the milk. Mix well. Beat the egg white until stiff. Fold in the egg white and the vanilla.

Pour the batter into the prepared tins.

Place in the preheated oven and bake for approximately 30 minutes, until the cake is done when tested with cake tester. Take care not to overbake.

Remove the cakes from the oven and set them on racks to cool. Cool them in their tins for 10 minutes, then remove them from the tins, peel off the waxed paper, and allow them to finish cooling. When the cakes have cooled completely, frost them with Boiled White Frosting (receipt follows).

Makes 1 cake, to serve 10 to 12

Boiled White Frosting

This classic frosting is delicious on Becky's Birthday Cake (preceding receipt) and on my Chocolate Cake (page 69). You may want to tint it a delicate shade of pink with a bit of maraschino cherry juice, and decorate the cake with fresh flowers for a festive touch. You must use newly laid eggs for assured success with this receipt.

> 2 farm-fresh egg whites, at room temperature
> 1 $1/2$ cups sugar
> $1/2$ cup water
> $1/2$ teaspoon vanilla extract

In a mixing bowl, beat the egg whites until they are very stiff but not dry.

In the top of a double boiler, over hot water, combine the sugar and the water. Place on the stove and stir until the sugar is dissolved. Boil *without stirring* until the mixture spins a thread when blown from a spoon — 242 degrees on a candy thermometer.

Add the syrup to the egg whites in a thin stream. This takes two people — one to beat constantly and the other to pour steadily. Add the vanilla and continue beating until the mixture reaches spreading consistency.

When the frosting has cooled sufficiently, you may ice your cooled cakes with it.

Makes enough to frost an 8- or 9-inch double layer cake or 24 cupcakes

Old-Fashioned Vanilla Ice Cream

In my early years, ice cream was almost always made at home, and then only for Sundays or birthdays. It was a tremendous treat, not only in the eating but in the preparation as well. It was a leisurely process, from getting out the cake of ice from the icebox and pounding it in a burlap sack with the maul, to making custard the day before and letting it cool in the trusty old icebox, to the slow turning of the freezer crank for the first few minutes. The entire family took turns cranking until this magical frozen dessert was done and the dasher was placed on a large Canton platter to be licked with delight. The cat and the dogs always got a share as well.

3 cups milk
1 1/2 tablespoons cornstarch
1/4 teaspoon salt
1 full cup sugar
3 farm-fresh eggs, slightly beaten
3 cups heavy cream
2 tablespoons vanilla extract

Scald a 1-gallon freezer can.

In a saucepan, scald the milk. In the top of a double boiler, over hot water, mix the cornstarch, salt, and sugar. Slowly add the scalded milk. Cook and stir for 8 minutes. Add the eggs and cook for 2 more minutes. Chill well in the refrigerator.

Add the cream and the vanilla and pour the mixture into the freezer can. Pack the freezer with cracked ice and salt and let everyone take a turn at cranking the handle, remembering to crank slowly for the first 5 minutes. Remove the dasher when the freezing is completed and pack the freezer with more ice and salt. Wrap it with blankets or newspapers and set it in the shade for several hours until you are ready to serve the ice cream.

Delectable!

Serves 18

Tasha's Chocolate Sauce

When it comes to my cooking and gardening, I have no modesty, and I am quite proud to say that this is an original receipt. It is simply the best chocolate sauce. I love to make a batch of Chocolate Cookies (receipt follows) and then place a spoonful of heavy cream, which has been whipped and sweetened, between two cookies, arrange a few of these sandwiches on a pretty dessert dish, and refrigerate them for a few hours. When I am ready to serve them, I pour chocolate sauce generously over all. Give not a thought to the modern notion of "diets" when you partake of this dish! The sauce is also wonderful spooned over hand-cranked Vanilla Ice Cream (preceding receipt). Serve the sauce hot or cold, as you prefer.

¹/₂ cup light Karo syrup
1 cup sugar
¹/₂ cup heavy cream
2 squares Baker's unsweetened baking chocolate
4 tablespoons Hershey's cocoa
2 tablespoons (¹/₄ stick) unsalted butter
1 teaspoon vanilla extract

Place all of the ingredients except the vanilla in a saucepan and stir to mix. Boil over low heat for a few minutes, stirring until smooth. Remove from the heat and blend in the vanilla.

Makes approximately 1 cup of sauce

Chocolate Cookies

This is a "never-fail" receipt, as long as you use the ingredients stated: *real butter, heavy cream,* and *cake flour.*

1 cup (2 sticks) unsalted butter, softened
1 cup sugar
1/4 cup light brown sugar, packed
3 squares unsweetened Baker's chocolate, melted
1 teaspoon vanilla extract
1/2 cup heavy cream
3 cups cake flour, sifted
1 teaspoon baking powder
1/4 teaspoon baking soda
1/4 teaspoon salt

In a large mixing bowl, cream together the butter and sugars. Stir in the chocolate, vanilla, and cream. Sift in the dry ingredients and mix. Cover the bowl and chill the dough thoroughly to make it easy to handle. Then shape it into rolls approximately 1 1/4 to 1 1/2 inches in diameter by 10 inches long (the receipt makes 3 rolls). Wrap these individually in wax paper and chill for 1 hour.

Preheat the oven to 350 degrees F.

Cut the rolled dough in slices 1/8 to 1/4 inch thick and place the rounds on parchment-lined aluminum cookie sheets, allowing space for the cookies to bake. Place the cookies in the preheated oven and bake for 8 to 10 minutes, until crisp.

Makes 5 or 6 dozen cookies

Washington Pie

What pleasant thoughts this receipt brings to mind of Grandma Tudor's taking me to S. S. Pierce to purchase favors for the February 22 celebration tea party. This was in the days when S.S.P. was in its glory. The clerks wore frock coats, and a boy delivered your groceries to your door in a hamper. The favors would make any child giddy with anticipation: red, white, and blue snappers, candy baskets in the same colors, miniature hatchets, fake cherries that glistened beautifully, thirteen-star flags, and such an array of sweets! Oh, my! It was indeed an event to remember.

Washington's Birthday was celebrated religiously each year. I do not believe the holiday has come and gone since without the making of a Washington Pie by some member of my family. The "pie" is actually a delicate cake that has predominant flavors of cherries from the Kirschwasser and raspberries from the jam.

Washington and Colonel William Tudor, my great-great-grandfather, were friends. My ancestor served as General Washington's Judge Advocate General. My grandmother delighted in telling us how General Washington, William Tudor, and Lafayette had formed the Society of the Cincinnati. I recall studying the array of correspondence regarding the Cincinnati that lined the walls of Grandmother Tudor's lengthy hall on Beacon Hill, from Jefferson, the Adamses, Lafayette, and many other figures of the time. It certainly sparked my intense interest in the history of this country.

This cake is best if you refrigerate it for several hours before serving (or preferably overnight) to enhance its flavor.

½ cup (1 stick) unsalted butter, softened
1 cup sugar
2 farm-fresh eggs, at room temperature
1²/₃ cups unbleached flour
2½ teaspoons baking powder
½ cup milk
2 tablespoons Kirschwasser
1 jar (8 ounces) raspberry jam
confectioner's sugar to decorate

Preheat the oven to 350 degrees F. Cut rounds of wax paper to fit the bottoms of 2 8-inch round cake tins. Grease and flour the cake tins and paper.

In a large mixing bowl, cream together the butter and sugar. Add the eggs and mix until light. Sift in the flour and baking powder, alternating with the milk. Beat until light and fluffy.

Pour the batter into the prepared cake tins.

Place the tins in the preheated oven and bake for 25 to 30 minutes. When the batter begins to pull away from the sides of the pan, test for doneness with a cake tester. Take care not to overbake.

When the cakes are done, remove them from the oven and set the tins on cooling racks for 10 minutes. Then invert the cakes on the racks, peel off the wax paper, and allow the cakes to cool completely.

Mix the Kirschwasser into the raspberry jam.

Slice the cakes in half horizontally. Place one layer of the cake on a pretty cake plate and spread it generously with the raspberry jam mixture. Repeat the process twice more and then top with the fourth layer. Prior to serving, place a pretty paper doily on top of the cake, shake confectioner's sugar lightly over it, and remove the doily. This leaves an attractive pattern on top.

Makes 1 cake, to serve 10 to 12

B.V.T.'s Torte

Barbara Von Trapp was my daughter Efner's close friend at school. I believe this torte was actually Maria Von Trapp's receipt from Austria. It is absolutely the last word for a party or any other kind of celebration, and though a bit long in the making, it is well worth the time spent. Whenever we make it, Barbara comes to mind. She was so beautiful, just like Arthur Rackham's illustrations of Undine in de la Motte Fouqué's tale of that name.

$^2/_3$ cup unsalted butter, softened
$1^3/_4$ cups sugar
4 squares Baker's unsweetened chocolate,
    melted and cooled
$1^3/_4$ cups unbleached flour
$1^1/_4$ teaspoons baking soda
1 teaspoon salt
$^1/_4$ teaspoon baking powder
$1^1/_4$ cups water
1 teaspoon vanilla extract
3 farm-fresh eggs, at room temperature,
    beaten
chocolate and cream fillings (receipts below)
$^1/_2$ bar Baker's German sweet chocolate for
    garnish

Preheat the oven to 350 degrees F. Prepare four 9-inch round cake tins, if you have them. If you don't, bake in two tins and slice each layer in half horizontally.

In a large mixing bowl, cream the butter, then add the sugar and blend until light. Stir in the chocolate. Next, sift in the flour and other dry ingredients, alternating with the water. Add the vanilla and beat for 2 minutes. Add the eggs and continue to beat for another 2 minutes.

Pour the batter into the prepared tins and bake in the preheated oven for 18 to 20 minutes, until the cakes begin to pull away from the sides of the tins. Do not overbake.

Cool the cakes in tins on cooling racks for 10 minutes, then remove them from the tins to cool completely before frosting.

Chocolate Filling:
$1^1/_2$ bars Baker's German sweet chocolate
$^3/_4$ cup ($1^1/_2$ sticks) unsalted butter, softened
$^1/_2$ cup toasted almonds

In the top of a double boiler, melt the chocolate. Allow to cool and blend in the butter. Stir in the toasted almonds.

Cream Filling:
2 cups heavy cream
1 tablespoon sugar
1 teaspoon vanilla extract

Whip the cream in a copper bowl. When it is stiff, fold in the sugar and the vanilla.

To assemble the torte: place the bottom layer of the cake on a cake plate and spread it with half of the chocolate filling. Top with the next layer and spread with half of the cream filling. Repeat the process. *Do not cover the sides.*

Make chocolate curls with the remaining half bar of German sweet chocolate, shaving off thin bits of chocolate with a knife from the not-too-cold bar. Use these to garnish the top of the torte.

Refrigerate the torte for several hours, or overnight, before serving.

Makes 1 torte, to serve 10 to 12

Gingerbread

This was my grandmother Tudor's receipt. It, like cornbread, is best cooked in an old-fashioned cast-iron pan. It is soft, with crisp edges, not hard, "Christmas-tree" gingerbread. It is especially good split and buttered for tea or breakfast.

¹/₂ cup (1 stick) unsalted butter, softened
¹/₂ cup sugar
1 farm-fresh egg, beaten
1 cup light molasses
2¹/₂ cups unbleached flour
1¹/₂ teaspoons baking soda
1 teaspoon cinnamon
1 teaspoon ginger
¹/₂ teaspoon cloves
¹/₂ teaspoon salt
1 cup hot water
1¹/₂ cups dark
   raisins

Preheat the oven to 350 degrees F. Grease 2 iron cornbread pans (12 pieces each) or, if you do not have cornbread pans, two 9 × 9–inch square cake tins.

In a large bowl, cream together the butter and sugar. Add the egg and the molasses, then sift in the dry ingredients and mix the batter well. Add the hot water and beat until smooth. Stir in the raisins.

Fill the prepared tins or pans half full, place them in the preheated oven, and bake the gingerbread 25 to 30 minutes, until done.

Makes 24 servings

The Tasha Tudor Cookbook

Dady's Brownies

This is Dady's receipt. Frosted with Seth's Fudge (receipt follows) after they have cooled, these brownies can make any dieter throw his or her best intentions to the four winds of heaven. I prefer them without nuts, but you can add them if you wish. Cut the brownies into squares before frosting with the fudge.

> *4 squares Baker's unsweetened baking choco-*
> *late*
> *1 cup (2 sticks) unsalted butter, softened*
> *4 farm-fresh eggs, at room temperature,*
> *beaten*
> *2 cups sugar*
> *4 teaspoons vanilla extract*
> *1 cup unbleached flour*

Preheat the oven to 325 degrees F. Grease and lightly flour 2 shallow cake pans measuring 8 × 8 × 2 inches apiece.

Melt the chocolate in a saucepan. Add the butter and stir to blend. In a mixing bowl, combine the eggs, sugar, and vanilla. Stir in the melted chocolate and butter, then add the flour and mix.

Spread the batter in the prepared pans and bake in the preheated oven for approximately 40 minutes. Check the brownies 5 minutes or so before the end of the baking time: if they are beginning to pull away from the sides of the pan, they are done.

Remove them from the oven immediately and cool them slightly on a cooling rack, then cut them into squares.

Makes 32 brownies

Seth's Fudge

This is the very best fudge for filling Christmas cornucopias or frosting Dady's Brownies (preceding receipt). My oldest son, Seth, is tops when it comes to making this delightful confection. If you plan to frost brownies with the fudge, do not stir it until it is thick, but instead leave it in a runnier consistency. Place a piece of waxed paper under the rack on which the brownies are cooling and pour the fudge over all. Whatever may drip through makes delicious eating!

Be certain to pay strict attention to the cooking temperature, or you will end up with "chocolate cement" instead of creamy fudge.

2½ squares
    Baker's
    unsweetened
    baking
    chocolate
2 cups sugar
¼ teaspoon salt
⅔ cup heavy
    cream
2 tablespoons
    light corn
    syrup
2 tablespoons (¼
    stick) unsalted
    butter, softened
1 teaspoon vanilla extract

Butter a 5 × 9–inch loaf pan.

Chop up the chocolate and combine it with the sugar, salt, cream, and corn syrup in a heavy saucepan. Place this in the top of a double boiler over hot water. Stir the mixture every so often, until it is melted and smooth.

Place the pot directly over medium-high heat on the stove, doing away with the lower part of the double boiler. Cook, stirring occasionally, until ¼ teaspoon of the mixture dropped into a small cup of cold water forms a ball that you can pick up with your fingers. This is the "softball" stage.

Remove the pot from heat, add the butter, and cool slightly. Add the vanilla and stir vigorously until the fudge becomes thick and loses its gloss.

Turn into the buttered pan and cut into squares when firm. Cover the fudge tightly and store it in a cool place.

Makes approximately one pound

English Toffee Bars

This receipt was given to me by a person I met in Akron, Ohio, when I was there many years ago on a talk tour. The children especially liked the cookies and used to pack them in their school lunches.

1 cup (2 sticks) unsalted butter, softened
1 cup light brown sugar
1 farm-fresh egg yolk, at room temperature
2 cups unbleached flour
8 ounces (1 cup) chocolate bits
1/2 cup English walnuts, chopped

Preheat the oven to 350 degrees F. Grease a 10 × 13–inch baking pan.

In a large mixing bowl, cream together the butter, brown sugar, and egg yolk. Stir in the flour and mix well. Spread the dough evenly over the prepared baking pan.

Bake for 15 minutes or until lightly browned.

Immediately cover with chocolate bits. When the chocolate has melted, spread it with a knife and sprinkle with chopped nuts. Score and cut while still warm.

Makes 2 to 3 dozen cookies

Baked Custard

My daughter Bethany is the expert on custards; hers never fail to turn out satin-smooth, with not a bubble to be found. I am not as fortunate, alas. The main thing is a really slow oven, and water kept under the boil. A wood stove is best; if you let the indicator drop to the needed temperature and the fire burn down, you have the perfect heat for custards. A custard served with real maple syrup is certainly hard to beat.

> *1 quart fresh milk*
> *5 farm-fresh eggs, at room temperature*
> *1/3 cup sugar*
> *1/4 teaspoon salt*
> *1 teaspoon vanilla*
> *nutmeg for grating*

Preheat the oven to 325 degrees F. Butter an 8 × 8–inch shallow baking dish or a dozen custard cups.

In a saucepan, scald the milk. In a mixing bowl, beat the eggs slightly. Stir in the sugar, salt, and milk. Add the vanilla and beat again. Pour the mixture into the prepared baking dish or cups, grate nutmeg over the top, and set in a pan of hot water 1 inch deep.

Cook in a 325-degree oven for 15 minutes, then lower the heat to 300 degrees for 1 hour, or until a knife inserted 1 inch from the edge comes out clean. Remove from the oven.

Allow the custard to stand and cool slightly before you cut it into squares or spoon it into dessert dishes to serve. Serve in custard cups on dessert plates, or unmold the cups onto dessert plates.

Serves 12

Coffee Jelly

This was one of my mother's favorites, served with Jersey cream, whipped and sweetened. While on the subject of jelly, I am surprised to say that I have never seen it in a receipt book other than the early editions of Fannie Merritt Farmer's. It is a real treat. The Coffee Jelly may also be served with mocha ice cream rather than whipped cream. Invariably it pleases guests and brings the cook compliments.

2 tablespoons Knox plain gelatin
1/2 cup cold water
1 cup boiling water
1/3 cup sugar
2 cups boiled coffee
1/2 pint heavy cream

Soak the gelatin for 20 minutes in the cold water, then add the boiling water and allow it to stand for several minutes to dissolve. Add the sugar and coffee. Turn into a jelly mold and chill thoroughly for several hours until firm.

Unmold the jelly onto a pretty serving platter and serve with whipped heavy cream.

Serves 6

Lemon Jelly

This is just the thing if one is feeling frail or in a delicate condition. Along with tea or ginger ale, it will soothe most invalids. However, it is also a welcome dessert with sponge or angel cake.

1 cup cold water
2 tablespoons Knox plain gelatin
2 cups boiling water
³/₄ cup sugar
¹/₂ cup freshly squeezed lemon juice
pinch salt

In a mixing bowl, add the cold water to the gelatin and stir. Let stand for a few minutes, then add the boiling water and sugar. Stir well to dissolve the gelatin. Add the lemon juice and salt.

Put the gelatin mixture in a pretty mold before you set it to chill for an attractive presentation.

Chill for several hours, until firmly set, before serving.

You can also make Orange Jelly in this same fashion. The ingredients are as follows:

¹/₂ cup cold water
2 tablespoons Knox plain gelatin
1 cup boiling water

³/₄ cup sugar
2 cups freshly squeezed orange juice
2 tablespoons freshly squeezed lemon juice
pinch salt

Follow the directions given above for Lemon Jelly.

Both receipts serve 6 to 8

Stillwater Iced Tea

This is one of my specialties of which I am inordinately proud. You must start with real tea, made correctly — that is, with freshly boiled water steeped for no more than five minutes. Fresh spearmint is another must.

The first pitcher of iced tea is marked yearly on the kitchen door where I keep all important records, including births, deaths, marriages, goat-kid arrivals, corgi whelpings, goings as well as comings home, first frosts, first snows, sightings of birds in the springtime, and so on. I never fail to mislay paper records, but a wall is not to be lost. To prove to you that I know whereof I speak about the frailty of paper notes, my parrot, Captain Pegler, once ate my town tax bill! "Useful bird," the town clerk remarked. "I wish he would eat mine!"

1 cup sugar
$1/_4$ cup water
5 tablespoons either English or Irish
   Breakfast loose-leaf tea
1 quart fresh, cold water
6 fresh oranges
6 fresh lemons
6 fresh limes
1 quart ginger ale
fresh spearmint sprigs for garnish

To make the sugar syrup, place the sugar and $1/_4$ cup water in a saucepan. Bring just to a boil and simmer until the sugar dissolves. Remove from the flame and place the sugar syrup in a canning jar. Allow it to cool before placing a lid on it. Keep the syrup at room temperature, as it will congeal in the refrigerator.

Put the cold water in a saucepan and bring to a boil. Place the tea leaves in a large pitcher and pour the boiling water over them. Steep for 5 minutes, stirring once. Pour off the tea through a strainer, into another pitcher. Allow it to cool but *do not* put it in the refrigerator, as the cold will cloud the tea.

Allow the juice of half an orange, half a lemon, and half a lime per glass — squeezed, of course, and strained.

For each serving, put the fruit juice in a large glass, 10 ounces or so, pour in the tea to half-fill the glass, and then fill the remainder with ginger ale and 2 ice cubes. Add sugar syrup to taste. Place a sprig of fresh spearmint in each glass and serve.

Serves 6–12

Tom's Stillwater Punch

This punch was invented by my younger son, Tom, who was quite a fine cook by the age of ten. It is a must for extra-special summer parties. We hold our Stillwater Party at the time of the Summer Equinox, inviting fifty guests for a splendid cold repast, Tom's Punch, a marionette show, and a lively square dance. You will probably want to double the quantity given here, as there is never enough if you fail to. Squeezing the fruit is quite a chore, so enlist two stalwart helpers if you can.

juice of 2 oranges, strained
juice of 2 lemons, strained
juice of 2 limes, strained
1¼ cups sugar, divided
1 quart cold black tea
4 sprigs fresh spearmint
3 cups freshly squeezed orange juice, strained
1 cup freshly squeezed lemon juice, strained
1 cup pineapple juice

1 cup raspberry syrup (receipt follows)
1 cup water
block of ice
1 quart ginger ale
fresh spearmint sprigs for garnish

Mix the juice of 2 oranges, 2 lemons, and 2 limes with 1½ cups of the sugar. Add the tea to this mixture, then add the 4 sprigs of fresh spearmint. Set aside to cool.

Mix the remaining orange and lemon juice with the pineapple juice and the raspberry syrup. Add this to the tea.

Boil the remaining ¼ cup of sugar with 1 cup of water for 5 minutes. Stir this into the tea mixture. Chill thoroughly. Serve over a block of ice in a punch bowl, adding the ginger ale at the last moment. Fresh sprigs of spearmint look pretty and add flavor floated on top.

Serves 30

Raspberry Syrup

4–6 quarts fresh raspberries
2 cups sugar
1 1/2 cups water
2 cups light Karo syrup

This receipt requires four to six quarts of fresh raspberries. I grow them in my garden, so this poses no problem. Add more sugar than you think is good for you, and a bit of water — say, 1 1/2 cups. Place in a *large* pan and bring to a boil, stirring constantly. I advise reading a book while stirring so as not to waste time.

Next, strain overnight through a jelly flannel. Be certain to cover the juice with a screen during the night, just in case a questing mouse should drown himself — very upsetting!

The next morning, heat the juice to a boil again, add the 2 cups of light Karo syrup, and pour the mixture boiling hot into scalded jars. Process in a hot water bath for 20 minutes. The syrup should be thick and extremely sweet, as it is only to be used in a diluted state.

Hot Chocolate

Hot chocolate makes a wonderful winter treat for cold days after sledding or skating. Winter being long, it is enjoyable to have particular treats such as this. It is especially good fun to have a fire outdoors and heat the chocolate over it. We frequently took a large basket with tin cups, a hanging pot, marshmallows, matches, and a tin milk carrier into which we had poured the hot chocolate. We would build a fire of birch bark down by the river and hang the pot over the fire to warm it.

3 cups milk
2 squares Baker's unsweetened chocolate
¹/₄ cup sugar
few grains salt
1 cup boiling water
1 teaspoon vanilla extract
¹/₂ pint heavy whipping cream

In a saucepan, scald the milk. Over hot water, melt the chocolate in the top of a double boiler. Stir in the sugar and salt, add the cup of boiling water very gradually, and stir until smooth. Then boil for 5 minutes.

Add this mixture to the scalded milk and beat it with a whisk until foamy. Stir in the vanilla and serve in a pretty chocolate pot that you have warmed with boiling water. Whip the cream and spoon a bit on top of the chocolate as you serve each cup.

Makes six 6-ounce servings

Old-Fashioned Chocolate Soda

Sodas are great fun for events such as birthday parties. The children enjoy making their own, but watch the boys with the soda water, as soda-pop battles quickly ignite!

Be sure to use a really good-quality ice cream, or better yet homemade, for truly delicious sodas.

2 tablespoons Hershey's chocolate syrup
1 quart club soda, chilled
1 or 2 scoops chocolate ice cream

In a 10-ounce glass combine the chocolate syrup with a bit of club soda. Stir to blend. Add the ice cream. Shake the soda bottle, holding your thumb over the mouth of the bottle, and squirt the soda into the glass. This allows you to make proper bubbles. Stir gently and add a sipping straw.

Serves 1

Lemonade

What a treat this is when served in a pretty glass with a sprig of mint! It was always a favorite at church suppers and country fairs at a few cents a glass.

I recall that in Nahant, at church bake sales, lemonade was sold at a stand by a jovial farmer's wife who wore a white mob cap and a large blue-and-white-checked apron. The lemonade was contained in an immense stoneware crock with a spigot at the bottom, and also in a very large salt-glaze pitcher with blue flowers on it. Chunks of ice and slices of lemons floated on top.

8 lemons, at room temperature
$^1/_2$ cup sugar syrup
2 quarts cold water
ice cubes
fresh spearmint sprigs

Roll the lemons to soften them, then squeeze them and strain the juice to remove the pits. Pour the juice into a pretty pitcher, add the sugar syrup and water, and stir well. Taste for desired sweetness, then chill until ready to serve.

Pour over ice in clear glasses and garnish with a sprig of fresh spearmint and a sipping straw.

Serves 8

CHRISTMAS
TREATS

Christmas Cookies

This is a German receipt given to me years ago by Louise Schade, the mother of my daughter Bethany's best friend, Inge Schade. I always make these at Christmas to have for tea and to give away in pretty boxes, which we make from empty oatmeal or cornmeal cartons. We cover the cartons, which we usually cut down, with pretty paper, line them with pages from the *Spectator*, paste paper lace around the rims, and tie them with ribbon. You can also reuse chocolate boxes by covering them. I make two-inch fluted round cookies to put in the little boxes for gift giving, as they are the easiest to pack.

I have a large basket of my grandmother's cookie cutters. They are enchanting, especially the duck and rooster.

There is an eagle, too, and lots of hearts, half moons, and so on. My son Seth, at the age of ten, cut a superb horse from a Danish ham tin. And friends, knowing my penchant for corgi dogs, have made some very fine offerings. Cookie cutting with the family is indeed a pleasant event.

2 tablespoons milk
1 teaspoon baking soda
1 pound (4 sticks) unsalted butter, softened
2 cups sugar
2 farm-fresh eggs
1 tablespoon vanilla
5 cups unbleached flour
$1/_4$ teaspoon salt
sugar for topping
nutmeg, freshly grated, for topping

Line 2 heavy-gauge aluminum cookie sheets with parchment paper.

Place the milk in a measuring cup. Add the baking soda and stir to dissolve. In a large mixing bowl, cream the butter. Add the sugar, eggs, and vanilla, then mix. Sift in the flour and salt. Add the milk and mix by hand until the ball of dough no longer sticks to the sides of the bowl. Cover the bowl and chill the dough for several hours.

Preheat the oven to 350 degrees F.

On a floured surface, roll out dough as thin as possible (a marble rolling pin works best) and cut out cookies with your best cookie cutters. Place them on the cookie sheets, leaving room for the cookies to spread as they bake. Sprinkle the cookies with sugar and a bit of freshly grated nutmeg before placing them in the oven.

Bake for 8 to 10 minutes, until nicely browned and crisp.

Yields 3–4 dozen

Mince-Pie Cookies

These are a great favorite with the gentlemen. To ensure crispness, store the mince cookies in their own tin or crock. Use the basic Christmas Cookie dough receipt (preceding receipt) to make Mince-Pie Cookies. In addition, you will need:

2-inch fluted round cookie cutter
unbleached flour
1 jar Nonesuch Mincemeat
sugar for topping
nutmeg, freshly grated, for topping

Preheat the oven to 350 degrees F.

On a floured surface, roll out the dough to 1/8 inch thick. Flour the cutter and use it to make 2 rounds for each cookie. Place half of the rounds on a cookie sheet, put 1 teaspoon of mincemeat on each round, top it with the second round, crimp the edges with a fork, sprinkle lightly with sugar and nutmeg, and prick the top with a fork as you would a pie.

Bake for 12 to 15 minutes, until the cookies are a delicate brown on the edges. Do not store with other cookies, as these will soften them.

Yields approximately 8 dozen

Hazelnut Cookies

These cookies greatly enhance Christmas gift boxes or platters of Christmas cookies. The red cherries make a pleasing spot of festive color.

You may use raisins in place of the hazelnuts. Simply grind the raisins as you would the hazelnuts, using the same quantity. To make Hazelnut Cookies, use the Christmas Cookie dough receipt (page 101), with the addition of:

3 cups hazelnuts
2-inch fluted round cookie cutter
nutmeg, freshly grated, for topping
sugar for topping
candied cherries

Preheat the oven to 350 degrees F.

Grind up the hazelnuts in a blender and mix them into the basic Christmas Cookie dough receipt. Roll and cut with a 2-inch fluted round cookie cutter as described above. Place the rounds on a cookie sheet, sprinkle them with sugar and nutmeg, and top each with half a candied cherry.

Bake in the preheated oven for 10 to 12 minutes, until delicately browned.

Yields approximately 12 dozen

Sandwich Cookies

You can make chocolate-filled sandwich cookies or chocolate-topped Christmas cookies by using the basic Christmas Cookie dough receipt (page 101). Just add:

12 ounces semisweet chocolate bits
2-inch fluted round or heart-shaped
*   cookie cutter*
sugar for topping
nutmeg, freshly grated, for topping

Preheat the oven to 350 degrees F.

Roll out the dough as described above and cut it out in the fluted rounds or hearts. Place on cookie sheets.

Bake the cookies in the preheated oven for 10 minutes, until they are a delicate tan.

Now melt the chocolate bits in the top of a double boiler over hot water. Frost half the cookies with chocolate and place another cookie on top, making a sandwich, or leave them as individual cookies spread with the chocolate.

Next, make a cornucopia of writing paper, fill it with melted chocolate, and decorate the tops of the cookies to the utmost of your ability. Great fun! And absolutely delicious.

Yields approximately 4 dozen cookie sandwiches

Linda de Christopher's Thumb Cookies

These cookies were invented by Linda, my daughter's friend, who came to upholster two chairs and remained for eleven years, until she married, outdoing even the "man who came to dinner."

She and I were in New York City and bought a bag of cookies at a famous bakery on Third Avenue. They were superb. I said to Linda, "Why couldn't we make some even better?" Clever Linda made up the following receipt all on her own.

1 cup (2 sticks) unsalted butter, softened
1/2 cup sugar
1/4 teaspoon salt
2 farm-fresh egg yolks, at room temperature, beaten
2 cups unbleached flour, sifted

1/2 teaspoon almond extract
1 jar (8 ounces) raspberry jam

Preheat the oven to 350 degrees F. Line 2 cookie sheets with parchment baking paper.

In a large bowl, mix together all the ingredients except the raspberry jam, in the order given. Roll the dough into teaspoon-size balls and make indentations with your thumb; fill the indentations with raspberry jam.

Bake in the preheated oven for 10 to 15 minutes, until delicately brown. Remove from the oven and place on a rack to cool.

Makes 6 dozen

Christmas-Tree Gingerbread

I use this sturdy gingerbread for making tree ornaments or gingerbread houses, but it makes for rather dull eating. You can either make your own shapes or obtain stiff cardboard templates of the animal ornaments I make for Christmas through my shop, the Jenny Wren Press. Some of my ornaments adorned the White House Christmas tree during the Johnson administration. You can also use this receipt to make a gingerbread house by baking slabs for the sides and the roof. It is a good idea to prick holes where you wish to sew the walls together when baked. I then use white boiled frosting for the snow and decorations, but use your imagination. Set the house on a mirror for the effect of a lake, and arrange spruce and other twigs for a forest. A splendid spectacle lovely to behold in a darkened room is created by lighting small candles around the shore of the mirror lake.

1 cup (2 sticks) unsalted butter, softened
1 cup dark brown sugar
3 farm-fresh eggs, well beaten
1 1/2 cups molasses
6 cups unbleached flour
1 1/2 tablespoons ginger
2 1/2 teaspoons salt
1 1/2 teaspoons baking soda
1 teaspoon cinnamon

In a mixing bowl, cream the butter and add the brown sugar, eggs, and molasses. Sift together all the dry ingredients and add them to the butter mixture. Mix thoroughly and chill well before rolling out on floured slab.

Preheat the oven to 350 degrees F and grease a cookie sheet.

Cut the desired ornament shapes 8–12 inches high. Place them on the greased cookie sheet and bake them in the preheated oven for 20–30 minutes, or until the gingerbread is very hard.

Makes approximately 10 large animal figures

Pineapple Upside-Down Cake

This Christmas specialty is very festive-looking and makes a nice gift when packed in a tin. Or, if you are ambitious, you can make charming cardboard bandboxes covered with dollhouse wallpaper in which to place the cake. Very pretty! This is my son Seth's favorite Christmas dessert.

Topping:
6 tablespoons sugar
1/4 cup (1/2 stick) unsalted butter
2 tablespoons pineapple juice
1 medium can (20 ounces) pineapple rings
1/2 cup or so candied cherries

Combine the sugar, butter, and pineapple juice in a 9-inch heavy iron frying pan. Heat slowly until the butter is melted and the sugar is dissolved. Remove the pan from the heat and add the pineapple rings in an overlapping arrangement. Decorate the holes in the center of the pineapples with candied cherries and set aside while you make the cake.

Cake:
1/2 cup (1 stick) unsalted butter, softened
grated rind and juice of one orange
1/2 cup sugar
2 farm-fresh eggs
1 1/4 cups unbleached flour, sifted
1 1/4 teaspoons salt
2 teaspoons baking powder

Preheat the oven to 350 degrees F.

Cream the butter with the grated orange rind. Add the sugar and beat until fluffy. Beat in the eggs, one at a time, and continue beating for 2 minutes. Add the sifted flour, salt, baking powder, and orange juice and mix well. Spoon the cake batter onto the pineapple in the pan.

Bake in the preheated oven for 40 to 45 minutes.

If you are using a wood stove, bake for 1 1/4 hours at medium heat. This cake is especially good baked in a wood stove. When the cake is done, turn the pan upside down, leaving it on top of the cake for a few minutes to allow the topping mixture to run down the sides.

Serve warm with whipped cream.

Serves 8

Dundee Cake

When November comes we start the Dundee cakes, as they are much improved by a stint in the freezer. This particular receipt was given to me by Dady. I believe it was her mother's in Scotland. We have made them ever since I can remember, so they are a family tradition. On December 6, the birthday of Saint Nicholas, they appear on the tea table without fail.

In making Dundee cakes, you need to enlist members of the family with strong arms, as the batter must be stirred for five minutes after the addition of each egg. The cakes make splendid gifts wrapped in foil and tied with red ribbon.

1 cup (2 sticks) unsalted butter, softened
2/3 cup sugar
4 farm-fresh eggs, at room temperature
2 tablespoons freshly squeezed orange juice
1 teaspoon vanilla extract
1/2 cup almonds, blanched and chopped
2 1/2 cups cake flour
1/2 teaspoon salt
1 teaspoon baking powder
1 cup dark raisins
1 1/2 cups currants
1/2 cup citron, chopped
1/2 cup candied cherries
whole blanched almonds and candied cherries
    for decoration

Preheat the oven to 275 degrees F. Grease and flour two 4 1/2 × 9–inch loaf pans.

In a large mixing bowl, cream the butter. Add the sugar slowly, mixing well as you do so. Add the eggs, one at a time, beating for 5 minutes after each addition. Stir in the orange juice, vanilla, and almonds.

Sift the flour together with the salt and baking powder into a large mixing bowl. Add the fruit and mix it by hand until it is well floured. Add the fruit to the first mixing bowl and mix thoroughly.

Pour the batter into the prepared loaf pans. Decorate the tops of the cakes with the extra almonds and cherries to form a pretty pattern.

Bake for 1 hour in the preheated oven. Check for doneness with a toothpick, taking care not to overbake. When the cakes are done, cool them in pans on cooling racks for 10 minutes before removing them from the pans to cool completely.

When cool, wrap in aluminum foil and freeze.

Makes 2 medium loaves

Christmas Tea Ring

This is very fine for Christmas breakfast, served with tea or coffee, and I almost always make it for this special event. It is a great favorite of my seven grandsons.

$1/_2$ cup milk, lukewarm
$1/_2$ cup sugar
1 teaspoon vanilla extract
$1/_2$ teaspoon ground cardamom
4 packages active dry yeast
12 farm-fresh egg yolks, at room temperature
4 to 6 cups unbleached flour, sifted

1 teaspoon salt
2 cups (4 sticks) unsalted butter, softened and divided
1 cup marzipan, softened
1 cup dark raisins
$1/_2$ cup pecans, chopped
1 cup candied cherries
$1/_2$ cup candied citron, chopped
1 cup confectioner's sugar
hot water

In a mixing bowl, add the milk, sugar, vanilla, and cardamom to the yeast and blend very well. Beat in the egg yolks. Stir in enough flour to make a medium-soft dough, then add the salt and work in 1 cup of the butter.

Knead the dough on a floured surface for 10 minutes, adding more flour as needed. When dough is kneaded enough, it will be shiny and elastic and will have small blisters on the surface. Place the dough in a well-greased bowl and turn it once to butter the top. Cover with a warm towel and set in a draft-free place to rise for 1 hour or so. The dough must double in bulk.

Punch the dough down and knead it briefly. Cover it and let it rest for 10 minutes. Divide the dough in 2 to 6 pieces and roll each into a long rectangle. Cream the marzipan with the remaining 1 cup of butter. Spread the marzipan mixture on the dough and sprinkle it lavishly with the raisins, chopped pecans, candied cherries, and citron. Roll the dough up lengthwise, pinch all the edges together with your fingers, and shape each length into a ring. Place the rings on a baking sheet, slash them with scissors, and brush them with melted butter. Cover them and allow them to rise until they have doubled in bulk, 45 minutes to 1 hour.

Preheat the oven to 350 degrees F.

Bake the rings in the preheated oven until they are nicely browned, 25 minutes or so. The baking time will vary depending on the size of the rings. Take care not to overcrowd the oven; leave ample space for air flow. You may leave some of the unbaked rings covered in a cool place, out of the draft, while you are baking others. Cool the baked rings on racks.

When the rings are cool, frost them with confectioner's sugar, mixed with enough hot water to make an easy spreading consistency.

Makes 2 large or 6 smaller rings

Tom's Pralines

We are always in need of sweets to fill the homemade cornucopias that grace the tree. These pralines, along with pieces of Seth's Fudge (page 86) wrapped individually in waxed paper, are very good fillers.

1 cup light brown sugar
$^1/_2$ cup Vermont maple syrup
$^1/_3$ cup heavy cream
1 tablespoon unsalted butter
$^3/_4$ cup pecans, coarsely chopped

In a saucepan, combine the sugar, maple syrup, cream, and butter. Place the pan over low heat and stir until the sugar is dissolved. Cook to the softball stage, or 134 degrees on a candy thermometer.

Remove the mixture from the heat and let it stand for 5 minutes *without stirring.*

Add the pecans and stir until the mixture is slightly thick and beginning to look cloudy. Drop it by spoonfuls onto waxed paper. Let it stand until cold and firmly set.

Store in a tightly covered container.

Makes approximately seven 4-inch patties or 2 dozen 1-inch patties

The Tasha Tudor Cookbook

Christmas Taffy Pull

A good old-fashioned taffy pull was a much-anticipated affair at our house each Christmas. The finished taffy wrapped in waxed paper is another cornucopia filler. Each child is allowed one cornucopia and one gingerbread animal from the tree.

1 cup brown sugar
2 cups molasses
1 tablespoon unsalted butter
1 tablespoon vinegar
1 teaspoon baking soda

Place the brown sugar, molasses, butter, and vinegar in a large, heavy-bottomed saucepan. Mix well and boil until the mixture hardens when some is dropped into a cup of cold water. This should happen when the candy thermometer is at 256 degrees. Then add the baking soda.

Turn the mixture onto a greased pan to cool. When it is cool enough to handle, grease your fingers with butter and pull the taffy until it is white and firm. The fun comes in sharing the task. Draw it into slightly twisted sticks and cut it into 1-inch lengths. Wrap each piece in waxed paper.

Makes approximately 1 pound

Priscilla's Butter Toffees

When you wrap these candies in colored cellophane, they make another festive addition to the cornucopias. Be sure to hang cornucopias out of corgis' reach — they find them very tasty!

1 cup sugar
$1/_2$ teaspoon salt
$1/_2$ cup (1 stick) unsalted butter
$1/_4$ cup water
12 ounces semisweet chocolate morsels
1 cup chopped nuts of your choice

Combine the sugar, salt, butter, and water in a heavy saucepan and cook to 285 degrees on a candy thermometer. Remove the mixture from the stove and pour it onto a greased cookie sheet to cool. Melt the chocolate bits and spread half on top of the cooled toffee. Sprinkle with half a cup of the chopped nuts. Cool, turn the toffee over, and repeat with the chocolate and nuts on the other side.

Makes $1/_2$ pound

Vanilla Cream Caramels

These are simply the best caramels, wonderful for filling the cornucopias. We make the plain cream caramels, but if you like you may add a half cup of chopped English walnuts with the final cup of cream.

2 cups sugar
2 cups dark corn syrup
1 cup (2 sticks) unsalted butter
2 cups heavy cream
$1/2$ cup English walnuts (optional)

Generously butter a 9 × 5–inch loaf pan.

In the top of a double boiler, cook over moderate heat the sugar, corn syrup, butter, and 1 cup of the cream, stirring constantly until the candy thermometer reaches 240 degrees F.

Remove the mixture from the heat and very gradually add the second cup of cream. Return to the heat and cook to 244–246 degrees F. Pour the mixture at once, without stirring, into the prepared pan.

When firm, about 3 hours later, invert the candy onto a wooden board and cut it into squares with a thin-bladed knife, using a light sawing motion. Wrap the candies in waxed paper.

Makes about 2 pounds, or 72 small pieces

Index

Index

Sources

A wide assortment of Tasha Tudor's creations—calendars,
Christmas cards, valentines, reprints of early miniature
books made for her children, replicas of her sketch books,
lithographs, paper dolls, and illustrated books—
are available from:
The Jenny Wren Press
P.O. Box 505
Mooresville, Indiana
46158